HAUNTED
STATEN ISLAND

HAUNTED
STATEN ISLAND

MARIANNA BIAZZO RANDAZZO

Published by Haunted America
A Division of The History Press
Charleston, SC
www.historypress.com

Garibaldi-Meucci Museum. *Photograph courtesy of Professor William J. Castello.*

First published 2024

Manufactured in the United States

ISBN 9781467156035

Library of Congress Control Number: 2024938196

To Gaspare, my unwavering protector,
I found solace in your shelter.
Your love, my shield against the dark.
Life was always an adventure, forever in my heart.

CONTENTS

FOREWORD

Staten Island is rich in history. A permanent settlement took place in 1661. Before that, the Lenape lived and prospered on the island. The island has also been known for the mix of ethnic groups and individuals who have settled therein. For these reasons and others, there are factual stories and fanciful tales of spirits and specters to interest those of a historical mind. Author, historian and educator Marianna Randazzo has once again filled the needs of those seeking knowledge. In *Haunted Staten Island*, she has woven paranormal tales with historical events. Many are new; others are as old as the lanes and byways of the borough. In fact, this new book takes up where Charles Hines and William T. Davis left off with *Legends, Stories, and Folklore of Old Staten Island*. Published in 1925, this missive focused on the north shore and wove together both tales and bits and pieces of the interesting, strange and peculiar. Some came down through the years by word of mouth, others in written form. Ms. Randazzo has done much the same but has brought us nearly up to date on uncanny and intriguing topics. Readers will enjoy this mystical walk through Staten Island history.

Patricia Salmon
author, historian
www.patsalmonhistory.com

ACKNOWLEDGEMENTS

In bringing this book to life, countless individuals' unwavering support and encouragement have been my guiding light. To my beloved children, Joseph, Jessica, Valerie, Kenneth, Gaspare and Melissa, who have stood by my side through every triumph and challenge, your love and encouragement have been my source of strength. To my beloved nieces and Joe Emerick, who always provide me with a great writing getaway, and to my cherished friends, you know who you are. You have all been with me through thick and thin, always offering a listening ear and a helping hand. I am endlessly grateful for your unwavering support. A special thank-you to my new friend Olga Topchii, photographer extraordinaire.

A special acknowledgment goes to Patricia Salmon, a remarkable historian whose passion for the history, beauty and lore of Staten Island ignited my curiosity and inspired me to delve deeper into the fascinating history of the borough. Your advice, presentations and books have been instrumental in shaping this book, and I am profoundly grateful for your invaluable contributions. Thank you to The History Press and my editors, who believed in this project.

To all who have contributed, big or small, to the creation of this book, I offer my sincerest thanks. Your support and encouragement have not only made this journey possible but also enriched it with your unique perspectives and insights. Your generosity truly humbles me, and I am deeply grateful for your contributions.

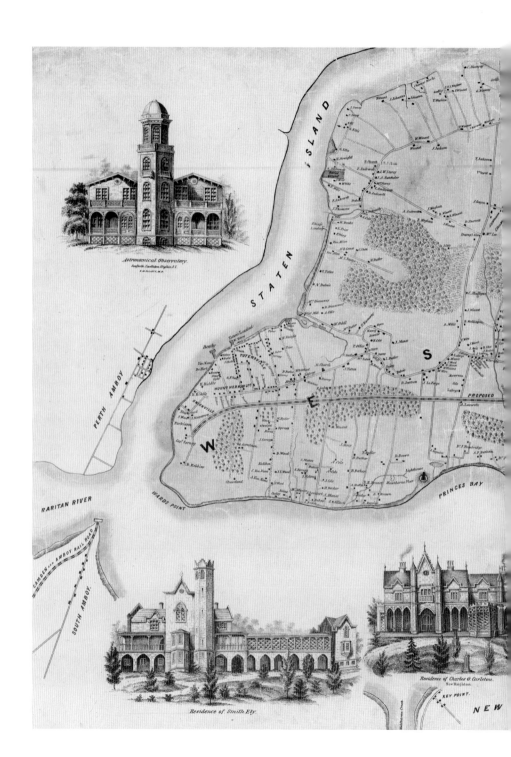

Astronomical Observatory.
Sanforth. Castleton Heights, S.I.

STATEN ISLAND

PERTH AMBOY

RARITAN RIVER

WARDS POINT

PRINCES BAY

CAMDEN AND AMBOY RAIL ROAD

SOUTH AMBOY

E

W

S

PROPOSED

KEY POINT

NEW

Residence of Smith Ely.

Residence of Charles G. Carleton.
New Brighton.

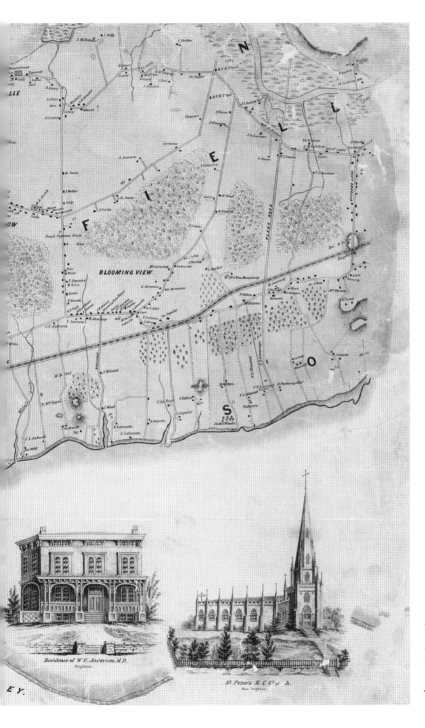

A map of
Staten Island,
originally
Richmond
County.
*NYPL Digital
Collection.*

INTRODUCTION

Everywhere I look, I see the news.
Is it real or fake?
—"People Are Strange," The Doors

Ghost tours have gained popularity in cities worldwide, offering a unique way to explore history and culture. Staten Island's paranormal stories, mysteries, urban legends and hoaxes provide an intriguing glimpse into the area's past and local culture, appealing to believers and skeptics alike. These tales transform tragic events into captivating stories and create unforgettable experiences.

The media, a powerful storyteller, wields significant influence over the perpetuation and contemporary interpretation of Staten Island's ghostly tales and legends. Various platforms, such as books, movies, television shows and online content, such as videos on YouTube, play pivotal roles in shaping the continuation and transformation of these tales, breathing new life into age-old stories.

They cultivate a sense of community around shared folklore, allowing for the exchange of personal experiences, interpretations and additional stories. This enriches the shared narrative and strengthens the bond among those who share a common interest in Staten Island's tales.

Yet it's essential to remain vigilant. While media amplifies and sustains these legends, it also has the power to distort or sensationalize the original stories, blurring the lines between fact and fiction. This is why a discerning eye is crucial when examining Staten Island's ghostly lore, separating historical truths from embellishments or fictional elements introduced by media adaptations.

Join me as we explore Staten Island's eerie folklore, mysteries, urban legends and ghostly legends and journey through its rich and haunting history.

Disclaimer: These stories are based on folklore, legends and personal accounts. Please remember that these are accounts and stories associated with these places, and individuals' beliefs in their haunted nature vary. While some people believe in the supernatural nature of these places, others may be skeptical. If you explore these locations, it is important to exercise caution, respect private property and follow applicable rules or regulations.

1

THE UNEXPLAINABLE

The universe is under no obligation to make sense to you.
—Neil deGrasse Tyson

In a big, mysterious world, some people believe that the dead linger, strange creatures wander and otherworldly visitors are drawn to us. The diversity of these entities, from ghosts to fairies and poltergeists to shadow people, is a testament to the vastness and complexity of the paranormal realm. Are there indeed ghosts, or should we refer to them as something less eerie, like unexplained entities? If such entities exist, shouldn't they be understandable through the laws of physics? On the other hand, how much do we really comprehend about the laws of physics? Do we believe we know everything about them? Certainly not! There is substantial evidence supporting the existence of these unexplained entities, challenging us to neither dismiss them nor label believers as eccentric. Therefore, we should expand our understanding of these entities until we can ultimately explain them using the laws of physics.

I'm seeing things, I'm hearing things, I'm feeling things I shouldn't.
—"Haunted," Beyoncé

"Graveyard Song" music sheet. *NYPL Digital Collection.*

WELCOME TO STAATEN EYLANDT: AN ACCIDENTAL DISCOVERY

We often discover what will do by finding out what will not do; and notably he who never made a mistake never made a discovery.
—Samuel Smiles

In 1609, the Dutch East India Company entrusted Henry Hudson with a ship called the *Half Moon* and set him on a mission to find a route to the Dutch East Indies. His original orders were to sail northeast, past the northern tip of the Scandinavian Peninsula, along the northern coast of Russia and eventually enter the North Pacific Ocean via the Bering Strait. However, fate had a different plan. Hudson, faced with freezing weather and ice blockage, was forced to change course. Little did he know, this deviation would lead him to a monumental discovery. Months into his journey, Hudson stumbled on a vast waterway, now famously known as the Hudson River. This accidental discovery would later play a crucial role in the history of exploration and trade. Staaten Eylandt was named for the Staten Generaal, or States General, the governing body of the Netherlands in the seventeenth century.

The Hudson River became a center of trade in the nation, forming a gateway to the west, thanks to Henry Hudson's accidental discovery. However, in June 1611, Hudson and his crew faced a harsh winter and dwindling supplies, which led to a mutiny that cast Hudson, his son and seven others adrift. They vanished, and the mutineers returned to England. Despite a trial, no one was charged with any crimes.

The fate of Henry Hudson remains a mystery and his story shrouded in speculation. A mysterious stone with the inscription "HH 1612 CAPTIVE" has fueled the belief that Hudson may have survived and lived among Indigenous peoples. Yet no conclusive evidence of this has emerged. Since the days of old New Amsterdam, locals in the Hudson Valley have reported seeing a mysterious ship with no known flags sailing down the river, seemingly defying the laws of nature. It moves against the tide and always appears to be without a crew. Within a few hours of its passing, powerful thunderstorms rock the area. The ship's origins are enveloped in mystery. Some believe it to be a remnant of the *Half Moon*, the ship Henry Hudson piloted on his journey up the river. Others speculate it is a ghostly apparition, a haunting reminder of the river's past.

Staten Island is known for its green park spaces, museums and historic buildings. It is often considered the "borough of parks" because of its numerous natural spaces. Beneath the surface of Staten Island's seemingly tranquil history lie many chilling tales. While Staten Island was designated a part of Richmond County in 1683, its ancient whispers and secrets remain in the twenty-first century. In 1898, the island, then still known as Richmond, was enveloped into New York City's boroughs. Though parts of the island remain a mystery, severed from the city's subway system, alternate routes to these spaces are available to the courageous traveler, and passage to Manhattan is accessible by the Staten Island Ferry. But amid the breathtaking view of Lady Liberty and the skyline of Lower Manhattan, one may sense the ethereal gaze of unseen watchers.

Journey forth, if you dare, for Staten Island's past is not easily laid to rest. Beyond the expressway bridges that tether it to Brooklyn and New Jersey, the island awaits, a province where history and mystery intertwine, where the boundaries between the living and the dead blur into obscurity. Stepping back into the 1920s, we encounter a Staten Island that was anything but forgotten. It was a dynamic center of life, teeming with distinctive cultural and historical features, all unfolding against the dramatic backdrop of Prohibition, jazz and the Great Depression.

The story begins with the Staten Island Ferry, not just a mode of transport but also a symbol of a city on the rise. Though it had ferried passengers since the eighteenth century, the ferry reached its zenith in the 1920s. Families

St. George Ferry, Staten Island, once took cars across the boroughs. *NYPL Digital Collection.*

would make grand affairs of their journeys on the ferry, packing picnics, donning their finest attire and embarking on a voyage across the harbor to the Big Apple. And no trip was complete without the children clamoring for a nickel's worth of ice cream from the vendors lining the terminal. Likewise, this author's ancestors cherished trips to Staten Island, then considered a haven for its beaches and countryside picnics, and of course, they loved the fabulous journey over on the Staten Island Ferry that docked at the Sixty-Ninth Street Pier. Unfortunately, the ferry was discontinued after the opening of the Verrazano-Narrows Bridge.

When prohibition is introduced, the code of criminality sets in.
—Desiderius Erasmus

Despite the nationwide ban on alcohol, Prohibition didn't quite catch on in Staten Island as it did in the rest of the country. The island was known for its speakeasies and secretive bars where people could enjoy a few shots away from the prying eyes of the law. Local lore has it that underground tunnels connected some of these establishments. Staten Island served as a fresh start for countless Italian immigrants, who carried slices of their homeland with them. In areas like Rosebank and South Beach, the scent of simmering homemade pasta sauce filled the air, embodying the essence of Italian cuisine. Italian Americans left an indelible mark on the island's culture, evident in the sight of Italian ice carts refreshing locals on sweltering summer days and the sounds of bocce games echoing in neighborhood parks. Sundays were sacred, as families gathered around tables to continue their old world traditions and, sometimes, superstitions that endured. The Great Depression left its mark on Staten Island, although its impact was less severe here than it was in the rest of the country. While the island's factories and shipyards experienced a downturn, the island's self-sustaining agricultural community acted as a buffer against the worst times. However, the economic slump fostered a sense of solidarity, giving rise to community initiatives and cooperatives to support one another through the hardships.

One of the most remarkable aspects of Staten Island in the 1920s was the community of Sandy Ground. Founded before the Civil War by free African Americans, Sandy Ground symbolized resilience and freedom. This community flourished in the '20s and was a crucial stop along the Underground Railroad. Its residents were oyster fishermen who brought a rich African American culture, interwoven with gospel music and southern cuisine, to the island.

Staten Island is still renowned for its strong sense of community, as evidenced by its mutual support and neighborly assistance during significant events like 9/11 and Hurricane Sandy. During 9/11, Staten Islanders were among the first to volunteer in rescue and recovery efforts, demonstrating remarkable solidarity and compassion. Similarly, when Hurricane Sandy struck, the island's residents came together to provide shelter, food and aid to those affected, showcasing their resilience and unwavering commitment to supporting one another in times of crisis. This enduring spirit of unity and cooperation continues to define Staten Island, making it a unique and supportive community.

2

HOMESTEADS, MANSIONS AND RESIDENTIAL HOMES

The oldest and strongest emotion of mankind is fear,
and the oldest and strongest kind of fear is fear of the unknown.
—H.P. Lovecraft

BILLOPP HOUSE, ALSO KNOWN AS THE CONFERENCE HOUSE
CONFERENCE HOUSE PARK
7455 HYLAN BOULEVARD

Staten Island's Billopp House, also known as Bentley Manor, is a grand stone mansion on a 1,600-acre property, built in or around 1680, making it one of the oldest homes in New York. It was constructed by Captain Christopher Bilopp, who was rewarded with 932 acres of land on Staten Island for his efforts in the Anglo-Dutch Wars, securing New York for Britain. Bilopp named his land Bentley Manor after one of his ships. The manor served as a wheat farm throughout its first century.

In August 1677, Billopp accepted an appointment as the collector of customs for Delaware. He resided in New Castle, Delaware, while his wife managed the property on Staten Island. In 1687, his land grant was increased to 1,630 acres, and it then became the Manor of Bentley. During the next few decades, Billopp traveled back and forth to England several times. He died in London in 1725.

The Old Billop House, erected in 1668, stands as a historic landmark, bearing witness to centuries of change and preserving colonial architecture. *NYPL Digital Collection*.

In 1702, Billopp put his two daughters, Mary and Anne, in charge of Bentley Manor. Mary married twice, each time to a clergyman, and had no children. Anne married Colonel Thomas Farmar in 1705 and resided in the manor house. The Farmars' third son, Thomas, born in 1711, assumed the name Billopp and inherited the estate. Thomas and his second wife, Sarah Leonard, had eight children; Colonel Christopher Billopp of Revolutionary War fame was their eldest.

Colonel Christopher Billopp (1737–1827), the eldest son of Thomas and Sarah Farmar Billopp, was born in the manor house and inherited the Manor of Bentley. He was known as the "Tory colonel" of the American Revolution.

During the war, Colonel Billopp was very active, receiving many communications and orders from those in authority, especially in 1777. Billopp commanded the Richmond County (Staten Island) Militia before the war and later commanded a regiment of native Loyalists. He was described as "a man of courage and energy, of high standing in the province of New York—of the Assembly of which he was a member for some years."

Colonel Billopp was active in enforcing the order that prohibited communication between Staten Island and New Jersey, and the Patriots of New Jersey were very hostile toward him, taking him prisoner on two occasions. His estate, Bentley Manor, was eventually confiscated, and on July 16, 1784, commissioners of forfeitures for the southern district of New York sold 850 acres of Bentley Manor to Thomas McFarren, a merchant. But Billopp had already deeded this property, including the manor house.

Billopp moved to Canada with his entire family except for his two sons, Thomas and John, who became businessmen in New York City. Colonel Billopp died on March 28, 1827, at the age of ninety at St. John, New Brunswick, Canada.

The manor house has two floors, an attic, a basement kitchen and a secret tunnel that was used for a peace conference between the British and Colonists during the war. However, the Conference House has another claim to fame: it's the scene of one of Staten Island's oldest ghost stories.

As early as the nineteenth century, locals claimed that the Billopp House was haunted. A caretaker who lived there during this time freely shared tales of the supernatural with visitors, taking particular care to point out a bloodstain on the floorboards that could not be washed out. It was believed that a murder had taken place there.

During the Revolutionary War, Billopp had turned his home into a hospital for British soldiers, smuggled them through the tunnel and buried the ones who died on his estate. His animosity toward the Patriots made him a target, and he was kidnapped twice. It was in December 1779 that Billopp was involved in a scandalous accusation. He accused one of his female servants of espionage in favor of the Colonists during the American Revolutionary War. As a signal, she would light a candle in an upper window whenever he was home. When Colonel Billopp discovered this plot, he flew into a rage and threw the girl down the stairs, resulting in her untimely demise from a broken neck. He evaded any formal accusations or trials for her murder, leaving justice unfulfilled. However, the echoes of this dark incident have lingered within the Billopp House's walls for over two centuries. The spectral presences of Billopp and his ill-fated servant continue to haunt the estate, their restless spirits intertwined in a tale of unresolved conflict and tragedy. Sightings of ghostly British soldiers add to the eerie ambiance, further shrouding the property in an unsettling aura of the past. Other legends report the apparition of a female spirit seen within the house and around the grounds. She is said to be the spirit of a young maiden who was wooed by Colonel Billopp. But when the colonel deserted her, she died of a broken heart. Those who have slept in a particular room of the house have reported being awakened by a sweet female voice singing a simple song.

Others have claimed they saw apparitions of Natives treading silently through the surrounding woods during the night. The area around the Conference House is also home to a site called Burial Ridge, a significant Native burial ground in the New York City metropolitan area. This prehistoric cemetery, the largest in New York City, was discovered at Ward's Point in Tottenville. Today, it is part of Conference House Park.

During the Revolutionary War, Billopp House was the site of the only official peace conference between the British and Colonists in 1776. Lord Richard Howe arranged to meet with Benjamin Franklin, Edward Rutledge and John Adams at Billopp House. Howe offered to end the war if the Colonists would swear allegiance to England. The four met in the house for three hours, but the conference ended without compromise.

Billopp House is reportedly haunted, with sightings of soldiers and a singing man and unseen touches. There's a residual haunting of a murder with sounds of shouting and screaming. The servant girl's grave is missing, and the exact number of ghosts in the home is unknown—except for one named Billopp!

The house is the only pre-Revolutionary manor house in New York City and was added to the National Register of Historic Places in 1982.

BILLOU-STILLWELL-PERINE HOUSE
1476 RICHMOND ROAD
DONGAN HILLS

Invisible things are the only realities.
—Edgar Allan Poe

The Billiou-Stillwell-Perine House is the island's oldest dwelling. Pierre Billiou built the original house in 1662. When the British took control in 1664, he transferred it to his son-in-law Captain Thomas Stillwell, who expanded it. The Perine family acquired it in 1760.

Margaret Perine, one of the last descendants to occupy the house, died in 1901. A story in the *Staten Island Advance* on October 27, 1976, reported that a psychic medium who conducted a séance in the spirited bedroom revealed the mystifying presence in the house was that of a young girl named Mary. Mary frequently visited the ailing Margaret. While returning home through the woods one day, Mary was assaulted and beaten. She died at her home a few days later. On her deathbed, she promised her spirit would remain

Above: The Billou-Stillwell-Perine House. *NYPL Digital Collection.*

Right: Alice Austen (here age twenty-two) was an iconic photographer who immortalized scenes with her camera. *NYPL Digital Collection.*

earthbound to warn visitors of impending danger. She pledged no one would be molested or hurt in those woods again. According to newspaper reports from the 1940s, yet another girl was attacked in the woods behind the house. Only this time, the girl survived because Mary's specter scared away the attacker. The victim also observed the guardian ghost. Although the medium communicated only with Mary, the curators felt several spirits inhabited the house.

Another tale says that in the 1950s, caretakers reported a "disturbing presence" in the home and said they often felt the eerie sensation of being watched. During the late 1960s, a famous ghost hunter and hypnotist investigated the happenings at the Perine House. He concluded that the spirit of a murdered girl haunted the property, calling the apparition "the girl in the garden."

In a bid to quell the terrifying occurrences, the valiant caretakers of the Perine House claimed they struck a deal with the home's resident ghost. A 1977 *Daily News* article recounts one caretaker's courageous words: "All of a sudden, I felt a chill, and I knew she was there. I told her that if she scared me out of the house, it would fall to ruin, and I suggested that we work together to preserve it."

In the early 1900s, it housed the Box Tree Tea Room, run by Alice Austen and Gertrude Tate. Today, maintained by Historic Richmond Town, the house is occasionally open to visitors. It is designated a New York State landmark.

BIDDLE HOUSE
CONFERENCE HOUSE PARK
70 SATTERLEE STREET

Biddle House is a formidable Greek Revival mansion that was erected by Henry Hogg Biddle in the 1840s. Several spectral sightings have been made here, each whispering a tale of its own. Visitors recount encounters with slamming doors, phantom footsteps stalking empty corridors and disembodied voices emanating from deserted rooms. These unsettling phenomena have created intrigue around the Biddle House, which sits within the desolate expanse of Conference House Park, overlooking the murky depths of Raritan Bay.

The H.H. Biddle House is a landmark of New York City. It was constructed in 1845 and owned by Mr. Biddle, who operated a ferry service

An old postcard of the Bentley Street Ferry, Tottenville. *NYPL Digital Collection.*

between Tottenville, Staten Island and Perth Amboy. It served primarily as a mode of transportation to service his Biddle's Grove, a temperance-era summer resort on the then very rural island. The Perth Amboy Ferry began service in June 1860, offering passengers steamship service between New Jersey and Staten Island. A ferry slip was then located nearby at the foot of Bentley Avenue. The service between Perth Amboy and Tottenville was profitable, especially with the Staten Island Rapid Transit Rail. Even after 1928, when the Outerbridge Crossing connected Staten Island to New Jersey, the ferry remained popular because it was reliable. Finally, in October 1948, the *Charles Galloway* made the Perth Amboy Ferry's final regular trip to Tottenville. Over the next fifteen years, the Sun Rise Ferry Corporation provided scaled-back operations with smaller boats, but in 1963, that service was canceled as well.

The building is a surviving example of Greek Revival architecture, noted for its twin double-height porticos in the front and rear that reflect on the home's hillside waterfront location. Along with its French-derived spring or bell-cast eaves, widely used on Staten Island starting in the late seventeenth century, the home itself is one of a type that is rare in both New York City and New York State. The building showcases ongoing New York City Parks exhibitions, cultural programs and events for the public.

KREISCHLER MANSION
4500 ARTHUR KILL ROAD

Every kingdom divided against itself is brought to desolation, and every city or
house divided against itself will not stand.
—*Matthew 12:25*

Just off Staten Island's Arthur Kill Road, Kreischer Street leads to Charleston, Staten Island, an industrial district with stables, shooting ranges, haunted mansions and sunken ships. It's a unique mix of the Wild West and Gothic horror; there sits the last remaining Kreischer Mansion. This Victorian home is rumored to be one of New York's most haunted places, especially if you consider that it is haunted by memories of murder and death.

The Queen Anne Victorian–style mansion that sits empty on Staten Island contains twenty-five rooms and was built around 1885 by German immigrant and "brick factory baron" Balthasar Kreischer. The mansion is a testament to the family's legacy. However, the Kreischer family's success was marred by tragedy, including the death of Balthasar and the destruction of the family's brickworks business. One of his sons later met a violent end within the mansion's walls. The Kreischer Mansion is said to be haunted by Edward B. Kreischer, who died by suicide after he shot himself in the right temple in 1894. Kreischer and his wife owned the brick business, and when the building burned down, it is believed that he was so distraught that it led him to end his own life. Contemporary newspapers immediately speculated that Edward's death had been caused by a falling-out he had with his brother. The two could not see eye to eye on how the family business should be run—or so it was claimed. In a diary entry, one family member wrote that he believed Edward had ended his life "over a woman" but did not identify her or elaborate.

The mansion is now rumored to be one of the most haunted places in New York, but it is still a remarkable piece of history that deserves preservation and appreciation. Despite the home's illustrious past, whispers of paranormal activity have long surrounded the Kreischler Mansion. Reports of ghostly apparitions, mysterious sounds and unsettling events have shrouded the property in mystery. Visitors and paranormal enthusiasts claim to have encountered shadowy figures, phantom footsteps, disembodied voices and inexplicable movements of objects within the mansion's walls.

A twin house, built for Charles's brother Edward, stood on the same property until its destruction in the 1930s. It quickly became a symbol of

Greenwood Cemetery, Brooklyn. Kreischler family burial ground. *NYPL Digital Collection.*

wealth and success in the area. Kreischer's brick manufacturing and housing construction spurred Kreischerville's growth. Early tenements arose in 1875, followed by double houses in 1890 on Kreischer and Androvette Streets. Designed by Peter Androvette, these wood-framed cottages symbolize the village's history. Today, four still stand on Kreischer Street, featuring sidewalks of yellow Kreischer brick, now New York City landmarks.

Though the Kreischer family had a large plot at the Green-Wood Cemetery in Brooklyn, Edward's body was cremated, his ashes sent to a cemetery in Queens. Kreischer's widow, who was reportedly prostrate with grief upon learning of Edward's death, remarried within eighteen months. People say they have seen a ghostly couple walking on the mansion's grounds at night.

Despite the mansion's magnificence, its reputation chilled in 2005, when a crime of unspeakable horror occurred within its walls. This incident cemented the mansion's eerie reputation and added a contemporary twist to its ghostly tales. In March 2005, an associate of a crime family was murdered in the house by a caretaker hired by the owner. The hitman, paid by the crime family, stabbed the victim, who then attempted to escape. Three other men caught and strangled the victim while the hitman continued to stab him. They drowned the victim, dismembered their body and burned it in the basement furnace. An FBI search of the property found bone fragments, personal effects of the victim and their blood. The hitman was sentenced to life in prison in 2008, and the organizer received a twenty-year sentence in 2009.

Despite its dark past, the mansion remains a landmark, recognized for its unique design. The mansion's haunting legacy lingers on as a reminder of the fragility of fortune and the darkness that can lurk within even the most beautiful places.

The Kreischler Mansion, also known as the Balthazar Kreischer House, is a historic landmark in the Charleston neighborhood of Staten Island, New York. As time passed, Kreischerville was renamed Charleston in response to anti-German sentiment during World War I. Meanwhile, the Kreischer Mansion stood watch on Kreischer Hill, becoming a New York City landmark in 1968.

The mansion's eerie reputation has not gone unnoticed. It has been featured in paranormal investigation shows and has fascinated ghost hunters who seek to unravel its spectral secrets. Various paranormal investigators and enthusiasts have explored the Kreischler Mansion, employing diverse methodologies and equipment, including EMF meters, EVP recordings, thermal cameras and spirit communication devices. Many claim to have recorded abnormal readings, captured audio purportedly containing spirit voices and documented visual anomalies on their equipment. The Kreischer Mansion was a filming location for HBO's period crime drama *Boardwalk Empire* and was featured on the reality TV series *Paranormal Lockdown*. In addition, actor Aaron Paul (Jesse Pinkman from *Breaking Bad*) visited the Kreischer Mansion during an episode of the TruTV series *Super Into*. The house is still used as the setting and backdrop for independent films.

HISTORIC OLD BERMUDA INN
VETERANS ROAD WEST

Empty chairs at empty tables,
where my friends will sing no more.
—Les Misérables

The Old Bermuda Inn stands proudly on Staten Island, a living testament to the passage of time. It holds the secrets of centuries past for those who dare to listen. This historic landmark, created by the esteemed Mesereau family in 1832, is not just a building but also a portal to a bygone era. Its existence, steeped in mystery and intrigue, beckons visitors from afar, and it is a great place to gather with friends and family.

Central to the inn's allure is the heart-wrenching tale of Martha Mesereau, a widow left alone as her husband marched off to battle in the Civil War. Martha diligently sat and waited every day after her husband left. Their correspondence brought hope as he described the trials and tribulations on the battlefield. She wrote back to him every time, telling him about the events on Staten Island. For months, Martha anxiously awaited his letters that reassured her he was alive and well. And then they stopped. But she did not stop waiting for him. Days turned into weeks and then months and years. Though rumors spread throughout the town and news of the war often looked bleak, Martha never gave up hope. She hoped her husband would return so they could have their own family one day. Even after the war ended, she waited by the window hoping that he would be one of those soldiers who showed up inexplicably. But her beloved never returned. It was in that house that Martha died, waiting for him. Martha's grief is said to have consumed her, binding her restless spirit to the inn.

Many have claimed they've caught fleeting glimpses of her spectral figure drifting aimlessly through the front area and dining halls, her ethereal form haunting windows and mirrors alike. Martha did promise her beloved she would wait at the window every day until he returned.

But Martha's legacy extends far beyond mere apparitions and whispered rumors. Immortalized in an oil painting displayed prominently in the first-floor hallway, her likeness is rumored to radiate with paranormal energy, a silent witness to the inn's haunted history. There was once a fire in a

Two Civil War soldiers in camouflage stalking the enemy in the forest. *NYPL Digital Collection*.

room where Martha's portrait stood, but it was untouched by the flames. Is this the spirit of her beloved finally coming home to his wife? Did he protect her image? Workers speak in hushed tones of inexplicable noises and door movements that defy logic, their accounts adding to the palpable sense of unease that permeates the home's atmosphere. Some say they heard the faint voice of a desperate man trying to find his way around the inn.

The tales of Martha's haunting have piqued the interest of the curious and drawn a legion of paranormal enthusiasts and investigators. These brave souls, driven by a thirst for the unknown, spend sleepless nights probing the inn's depths, searching for signs of otherworldly presences amid the shifting shadows and unyielding silence. Their experiences, a testament to the inn's haunted history, add to its allure and mystery.

Despite changes in ownership and function over the years, the Old Bermuda Inn remains a true source of historic charm and supernatural intrigue. In the 1980s, under the stewardship of John Vincent Scalia and George Burke, the property was transformed into an upscale restaurant, yet Martha Mesereau's ghostly legacy endures, woven into the very fabric of the inn's existence. The inn, a Victorian masterpiece that was once the parsonage of St. Luke's Church in the 1840s, was restored to its original grandeur and is now a beautiful guesthouse. Guests experience the timeless allure of the Old Bermuda Inn in the original portion of the building. Yet even amid the laughter and revelry, Martha's presence lingers, her watchful gaze seeming to follow visitors as they traverse the hallways, a silent reminder of the spectral secrets that lie buried within.

ALICE AUSTEN HOUSE, ALSO KNOWN AS CLEAR COMFORT 2 HYLAN BOULEVARD

How can the light that burned so brightly suddenly burn so pale?
—West Side Story

The Alice Austen House, known as Clear Comfort, is a renowned historic residence celebrated for its breathtaking view of the Verrazzano-Narrows Bridge.

Alice Austen, born in 1866 at Woodbine Cottage, moved with her mother to Clear Comfort after her father abandoned them. They lived with her grandparents on a property initially purchased by her grandfather John

Austen. Over twenty-five years, John transformed the eighteenth-century farmhouse into an attractive Carpenter Gothic cottage set amid meticulously landscaped grounds.

It was here that Alice's photographic journey began. She captured vibrant moments that depicted the essence of New York City, documenting its evolution, immigrant life, Victorian women and her extensive travels. Her focus on marginalized communities extended to commissions, including recording the people and conditions at immigrant quarantine sites in the 1880s. Alice's lifelong partner, Gertrude Tate, joined the household in 1917, despite Gertrude's mother's and sisters' disapproval. Gertrude spent twenty-eight years living in the house with Alice until they were evicted in 1945. Alice met Gertrude, a kindergarten teacher and professional dancing instructor from Brooklyn, in 1897 during an excursion to the Catskills.

Alice's notable ancestor, Revolutionary War hero Peter Townsend, added to the family's history. A link from the "Great Chain," manufactured by Townsend's Sterling Iron Works during the Revolutionary War, was a treasured possession displayed over the parlor fireplace.

During the Revolutionary War, when the British were stationed in Staten Island, a red-coated trooper of St. George supposedly loved a maiden who resided in the house. Local folklore tells the tale of a broken-hearted British soldier who, driven to despair, hanged himself from a massive beam. The tale suggests his spirit lingers, contributing to the reported ghostly encounters and eerie occurrences at the home.

When the Austen family purchased the farmhouse in 1844, Revolutionary War–era ghosts were said to be comfortably settled there. Despite believing the cottage was haunted, Alice remained there throughout her adulthood.

Facing financial hardships, particularly during the Great Depression, Alice and Gertrude were forced to leave Clear Comfort in 1945. While Tate and Austen maintained a close and loving relationship for many years, Tate's family disapproved of their partnership. This lack of acceptance was a significant factor in the couple's challenges, especially in their later years when financial and health issues compounded their difficulties. Alice declared herself a pauper and resided at what was once called the Richmond County Poor House. Tate moved in with her family in Queens. But despite the distance, Tate visited Austen weekly.

Historian Oliver Jensen rediscovered Austen's work in 1951, leading to her departure from the poorhouse with income from her photographic collection. Alice was then placed in a private nursing home. The final wishes of Alice and Gertrude were to be buried together.

Clear Comfort, the home of Alice Austen and Gertrude Tate. *NYPL Digital Collection.*

Alice died on June 9, 1952, and she was buried at the family plot at Moravian Cemetery in Staten Island. Gertrude Tate lived another ten years. The Tate family refused to honor the women's wishes to be buried together, so Gertrude was buried in Cypress Hills Cemetery in Brooklyn.

Legend suggests that Alice returned to Clear Comfort in the afterlife, joining the ghosts she once believed haunted her. Today, the Alice Austen House is a museum and National Historic LGBTQ site, preserving Alice's legacy as a pioneering American photographer.

These tales of ghostly apparitions and unexplained phenomena contribute to Clear Comfort's mystique, adding a layer of intrigue to the home's rich history.

THE GARIBALDI-MEUCCI MUSEUM
420 TOMPKINS AVENUE

Friendship is the shadow of the evening, which increases with the setting sun of life.
—*Jean de La Fontaine*

The Garibaldi-Meucci Museum is a historic frame cottage in Staten Island's Rosebank section. This was where Italian hero Giuseppe Garibaldi was a guest of inventor Antonio Meucci and his wife, Esterre. Garibaldi, renowned for his role in the Italian independence movement, stayed with Meucci, the inventor of the "teletrofono." Garibaldi, known for his military exploits in Europe and South America, played a significant role in the history of this museum.

The Gothic-style frame cottage, probably built around 1845 by Dr. William Townsend, stood on Ditson Street in Staten Island. The area had seen resort development since the 1820s. By 1850, theatrical promoter Max Maretsch was renting it, likely aware of Antonio Meucci's recent arrival from Havana. Meucci's housemate, Giuseppe Garibaldi, was also known to Maretsch.

Born in 1807 in Nice, Garibaldi initially pursued a seafaring life but later became a key figure in Italy's unification and independence movement in the 1830s. He fought in Brazil and Uruguay before returning to Italy in 1848 to battle the Austrians. Forced to flee after the Republic of Rome's collapse in 1849, Garibaldi's military feats earned him the title "hero of two worlds."

Garibaldi arrived in New York in 1850. He was unwell, and Meucci, financially stable from electroplating sword hilts in Cuba, offered assistance. The men shared a cottage and enjoyed water views, hunting and fishing. Garibaldi returned to Italy in 1854 to continue his fight for a constitutional monarchy, leaving Meucci some mementos, including his red shirt that he wore during the defense of Rome, which is exhibited in the museum today.

After Garibaldi's departure, Meucci faced setbacks. He experimented with various inventions, notably the "teletrofono," which he developed after he was inspired by observing voice transmission through wires in Havana in 1849. Over the next two decades, he refined the concept, eventually filing a preliminary patent application (Caveat) in 1871 for what he termed a "sound telegraph."

Meucci faced obstacles and deception due to his lack of English-speaking skills. Meanwhile, Alexander Graham Bell's patenting of the telephone in 1876 led to speculation of a conspiracy against Meucci. Despite Meucci receiving minimal recognition for his accomplishments, his house, once shared with Garibaldi, became a memorial after Garibaldi died in 1882. Meucci preserved Garibaldi's room; by 1887, hundreds of Italian visitors had paid homage there. Meucci died in 1889, and in 1906, his house was moved to its present site by the Garibaldi Society of Staten Island. An unconventional Pantheon-like structure was constructed over the house but was later removed.

The Garibaldi memorial, erected to honor Giuseppe Garibaldi, a hero of two worlds. *NYPL Digital Collection.*

The Garibaldi-Meucci Museum has been the subject of multiple paranormal investigations, several of which can be seen on YouTube. Staten Island native Jacqueline Downing, who specializes in spirit communication, told this author that she regularly communicated with the spirits between late 2010 and late 2017 and that she taped her conversations with them. Jacqueline says she became interested in the museum after attending a series of ghost tours organized by the Staten Island Paranormal Society in October 2010. Subsequently, during her visits, Jacqueline developed relationships with many of the museum's spiritual inhabitants, including the spirits of Antonio Meucci, Esterre Meucci, Giuseppe Garibaldi and household servants who worked there over the decades. "Despite any sadness and hardship in the house over the years, there was also playfulness and humor," claimed Jacqueline. She related witnessing one museum visitor, a little girl, get poked in the ribs by an unseen Mr. Meucci!

Friendship is the only cement that will ever hold the world together.
—*Woodrow Wilson*

THE PORTRAIT

Historian and artist Professor William John Castello shared his artwork and the following with this author.

In 1850, a quaint cottage nestled on the shores of the Hudson River in Staten Island welcomed two influential figures: Antonio Meucci, the renowned inventor, and Giuseppe Garibaldi, the future unifier of Italy. For a fleeting eight months, their lives intertwined within the walls of this humble abode, forging a bond that would endure a lifetime. Despite time, the cottage remains a tangible link to history, adorned with artifacts that narrate its significance. During a visit to this historic site, artist William John Castello, prompted by a lack of representation of the friendship between Meucci and Garibaldi, was inspired to create the only known portrait of the two men together.

A portrait of Meucci and Garibaldi, which is now hanging in the Garibaldi-Meucci Museum. *Courtesy of the artist, William J. Castello.*

Today, the portrait hangs in the cottage alongside cherished pieces of furniture crafted by Meucci and Garibaldi themselves. The intimate parlor's ambiance soaks in the imagined conversations of these historical figures, their presence palpable in the room.

Under the guardianship of the Order Sons and Daughters of Italy, the cottage has garnered tales of paranormal occurrences over the years, adding to its mystique. Yet whether haunted or not, the cottage remains a poignant time capsule, preserving the legacy of two remarkable individuals whose camaraderie continues to welcome visitors, transcending the passage of time.

Drawn by Harry Fenn from a photograph

THE MEUCCI-GARIBALDI HOUSE AT CLIFTON, STATEN ISLAND, AS IT IS TO-DAY

The Meucci-Garibaldi House as it stood in Clifton, Staten Island. *NYPL Digital Collection.*

3

RICHMOND TOWN

SNUG HARBOR, ROADS, LANDMARKS AND INDUSTRIES

SAILORS' SNUG HARBOR

The pessimist complains about the wind; the optimist expects it to change; the realist adjusts the sails.
—William Arthur Ward

Snug Harbor Cultural Center and Botanical Garden, once a retirement haven for sailors, now thrives as a cultural center. Founded in the early nineteenth century by Captain Robert Richard Randall, Sailors' Snug Harbor provided refuge for aging sailors who were weary from the sea. Amid struggles, residents often turned to alcohol and opium, leading to tragic deaths by suicide. Today, the site's old dormitories are rumored to be haunted, with reports of phantom footsteps, slamming doors and the scent of pipe smoke. Established in the 1800s, Snug Harbor grew from three buildings to over fifty, accommodating around one thousand seamen. Renowned for its inclusive policies, it became one of the earliest democratic charitable institutions in the United States.

The Matron's Cottage
Snug Harbor
1000 Richmond Terrace

The sinister reputation of Snug Harbor Cultural Center and Botanical Garden was thrust into the spotlight by the paranormal investigators of *Ghost*

A composite of illustrations representing Sailors' Snug Harbor. *NYPL Digital Collection.*

The front view of the main building, Sailors' Snug Harbor. *NYPL Digital Collection.*

Adventures, known for their in-depth exploration of the world's scariest and most notorious haunted places. A chilling tale emerges from the Livingston Cultural Center. According to the show's team, there's a story of a woman who kept her mentally challenged child confined in the basement while she was away from home. Tragically, one day, the child managed to escape, resulting in a horrifying incident in which the mother was killed before the child vanished without a trace.

The matron at Snug Harbor had a strict policy that forbade her assistants from mingling with the sailors. However, she broke her rule and had an affair with one of the retired sailors, Herman Ingalls. The *New York Times* reported the story on February 1, 1863:

> *At 9 o'clock yesterday morning, a most atrocious homicide was committed at the Sailors' Snug Harbor, Staten Island, under the following circumstances: The chaplain of the Institution, Rev. ROBT. A. QUINN, had been holding religious services in the Sailors' Chapel, and was on his return home, when a sailor named HERMAN INGALLS, who was standing near the corner of the main building, confronted him saying: "You'll expose me, I know you will, if you live," and immediately drew from his breast-pocket a double-barreled pistol and fired at Mr. QUINN. The ball entered his left breast immediately under the heart, and after reeling for a few seconds, Mr. QUINN dropped dead, exclaiming, "I'm shot! I'm shot!" The sailor then turned round, placed the pistol close to the side of his own head, discharged the remaining barrel, and fell. The shot tore away his entire lower jaw.*

The matron and Herman Ingalls had had an affair that resulted in a secret pregnancy. They couldn't go to the hospital for the child's birth, so the butcher assisted with the delivery. The baby was born with several congenital disabilities due to complications during delivery, and the butcher blamed himself. He began self-medicating with alcohol, causing problems in his marriage. One night, he was locked out, and rather than finding somewhere warm to spend the evening, he fell asleep on the front porch and ended up freezing to death.

Since the baby, a boy, survived, the matron and Herman hid him in the double-sealed basement of the Matron's House to keep his existence a secret. But as the boy grew, the couple worried about his future and who they could turn to for help. Herman decided to confide in the chaplain of Snug Harbor, Reverend Quinn, against the matron's advice. He fabricated

The chapel, Sailors' Snug Harbor. *NYPL Digital Collection.*

a story, claiming he had raped the matron and fathered her child, seeking to protect her from shame. However, Reverend Quinn doubted the credibility of Herman's tale, considering the pair's physical sizes. This skepticism led Herman to realize his error in confiding in the chaplain.

Herman left quickly but felt like their secret wasn't safe anymore. He thought the reverend would expose them. On January 31, 1863, Herman met the reverend before Main Hall C. According to the papers, Herman said, "You'll expose me; I know you will if you live!" Then he shot the reverend, turned the gun around and shot himself.

Well, Snug Harbor was in chaos, and the press was on their way over to investigate the shocking murder-suicide. The matron heard what Herman had done, but she wasn't sure who knew what about the boy, so she ran to her house and went down into the basement to ensure that he was still there and OK. But he had disappeared from the room. Later, she discovered him hiding between the doors. The boy had seen the outside world and refused to go back inside.

He resisted when the matron attempted to coerce him back into the basement. Despite her efforts, he reached a breaking point and lost control. After grabbing a pair of rusty scissors, he repeatedly stabbed the matron as she screamed for help, drawing the attention of others, who intervened. Upon realizing the severity of his actions, the boy tried to flee but was quickly apprehended by witnesses who saw him covered in blood. Mistaken for an assailant, he was swiftly lynched outside the Matron's House, with justice administered on the spot by his captors. Tragically, Herman, the matron and the boy all met their demise at Snug Harbor that fateful day.

In response to the murder-suicide, Snug Harbor's leaders panicked, fearing the repercussions of the story on their reputations. To avoid further scrutiny, they covertly buried the matron and the boy in unmarked graves at the nearby Monkey Hill Cemetery. Monkey Hill is the Snug Harbor cemetery located past the Matron's House. The cemetery is called Monkey Hill, a name that references a sailor's agility when climbing a ship's rigging. The precise location of their burial remains a mystery.

Several staff members who work in Main Hall C have shared their experiences of paranormal activity inside this historic building. Many have heard footsteps, keys jingling and doors opening and closing independently. They also see strange reflections, shadows where they shouldn't be and figures on the balcony when no one else is present. Main Hall C was the first building on the campus where many of these sailors once lived. Some believe spirits have formed a solid connection to the place. Tour guides at the Governor's House have mentioned that there have been many reports of paranormal occurrences at the house and that investigators have picked up voices on recordings telling everyone to get out.

The Music Hall
Snug Harbor
1000 Richmond Terrace

The Music Hall at Snug Harbor is known for its haunting history, with paranormal activity reported by staff and rangers. One of the prior directors of Snug Harbor also took a photograph of a concert in which there was an absence of pixels in the shape of a giant woman. Staff have wondered if this might have been the matron herself. There are tales of a playful ghost that favors balcony seats and can pass through doors effortlessly. A purple orb was once seen during a music rehearsal. In 2013, paranormal investigators organized a ghost hunt at Snug Harbor, but no ghosts were seen. Witness accounts attest to the eerie realities at Snug Harbor.

A staff member also reported seeing a little girl wandering alone in the Music Hall. When they went to help her find out where her parents were, the little girl ran away and disappeared as soon as she turned a corner. While it's not likely that the girl would have lived at Snug Harbor, it's possible she was a former member of the neighboring community. Many families came from off campus to attend church at Snug Harbor, and it's thought that perhaps she has some connection to the place because of that.

In 2013, the New Jersey Paranormal Research Organization (NJ PRO) guided twenty adventure seekers on a tour of the Music Hall at Snug Harbor. The hall, which dates to 1892, is renowned for its haunting history. Andy Rivera, the cofounder of NJ PRO, highlighted the eerie atmosphere of the Music Hall, citing unexplained mysteries from previous investigations. Although they did not witness any ghosts, some participants sensed a lingering presence. Once a skeptic, Rivera admitted a shift in belief, stating, "I definitely believe something's there."

The paranormal phenomena at Snug Harbor are too numerous for doubt, with a trail of witnesses who can reflect on the area's eeriness.

RICHMOND TOWN
441 CLARKE AVENUE

Every corner holds a story, every stone whispers a tale. In places steeped in history, the past is not just a memory but a living presence.
—*unknown*

Richmond Town in Staten Island boasts a historic village that features haunted buildings, including the Court House Hotel from 1858. Adjacent to it lies a graveyard that is rumored to be home to restless spirits. Visitors can explore year-round with self-guided and tour-guided visits and special events like candlelight tours.

Situated in the heart of the island, Historic Richmond Town has a rich history dating to the 1600s, when it was first settled by the Dutch. Transitioning to British hands, it soon became the county seat, hosting the island's inaugural courthouse and jail. In 1776, British forces landed on Staten Island as Congress declared America's independence. The island became a refuge for Loyalists and escaped enslaved people who joined the British army.

Despite a decline when the court was relocated to St. George, the town's legacy was preserved as it transformed into a historic village during the 1950s. The opening of the Verrazzano Bridge in 1964 marked a pivotal moment, connecting Staten Island to the rest of New York City and sparking significant construction that reshaped the island's landscape. Facing impending demolition, numerous historic homes found refuge in this site. Today, Historic Richmond Town is a sprawling "living history village and museum complex," spanning nearly fifty acres and showcasing thirty historic buildings.

Rumors persist that Historic Richmond Town is haunted, with spirits allegedly lingering in its buildings late at night. Visitors have reported eerie phenomena, such as footsteps, unexplained sounds, missing objects, cold spots and voices, making this an ideal destination for ghost hunters.

The Guyon-Lake-Tysen House
North Side of Richmond Road between Court Place and St. Patrick's Place

Would you know my name
if I saw you in heaven?
—*"Tears in Heaven," Eric Clapton*

In the quiet halls of Historic Richmond Town on Staten Island, sorrow lingers among the timeworn houses. Among them stands the Guyon-Lake-Tysen House, a somber relic of past homesteads, its walls heavy with the weight of tragedy. The house was built in 1740 by French Huguenot Pierre Guyon and now holds untold secrets. Its upper floors were left unfinished, a reminder of incomplete dreams. In 1820, the Lake family, descendants of the original owner, installed a kitchen, yet even this addition could not dispel the gloom that lurked within.

Elizabeth Lake Tysen, a daughter of the Lakes, became the focal point of the house's eerie tales. After marrying David Tysen, a prominent local figure, she was gifted the family farm, but Elizabeth's life was marked by hardship and loss. Her family, the Lakes, were known for their contributions to the local community, and their story is intertwined with the house's history.

Over the years, Elizabeth bore eleven children, yet the cruel hand of fate stole away most of them before they could blossom into adulthood. Once filled with laughter and play, the children's bedroom now holds only echoes of the past as toys mysteriously shift and footsteps resound in the empty corridors.

Visitors to the house speak of strange occurrences—a phantom presence, the sound of children's laughter and even the faint strains of a penny whistle drifting through the air. In the quiet of the night, the sorrowful tale

The Guyon-Lake-Tysen House, a testament to Staten Island's past, preserves history within its walls for generations to come. *NYPL Digital Collection.*

of Elizabeth and her lost children resonates, a haunting reminder of the fragility of life and the enduring power of grief.

Stepping into the Guyon-Lake-Tysen House, visitors are greeted by a portrait that holds a chilling secret. The portrait is said to be that of Elizabeth Lake Tysen—and her gaze is said to follow you. Her expression is rumored to change when captured in a photograph. Some claim her face bears the haunting marks of bruising. What tragedies befell those who once dwelled within these walls?

Situated initially on Tysens Lane in Oakwood, Staten Island, the house now stands between Court and St. Patrick's Places on the north side of Richmond Road. Moved to Historic Richmond Town in 1962, the home carries a past, a reminder of the lives that once graced its halls.

As visitors explore the house's darkened corners and hidden alcoves, the portrait in the east parlor watches silently. Its mysterious expression reflects the sorrow and secrets that lie buried within the walls of the Guyon-Lake-Tysen House.

The Voorlezer's House and Rezeau–Van Pelt Cemetery
Arthur Kill Road, Center Street

For never was a story of more woe
than this of Juliet and her Romeo.
—Romeo and Juliet, *William Shakespeare*

Rezeau–Van Pelt Cemetery no. 14 is a historic burial ground near Tysen Court. It contains a replica iron fence with intricate details, such as a gate adorned with an angel's head. This private cemetery served families associated with the Voorlezer's House and was designated a landmark in 1969. In the Dutch colonial era of North America, the term *voorlezer* held significant importance. Translating to "fore-reader" or "one who reads (to others)," a voorlezer was more than just a reader; they were dedicated pillars of their communities. From the mid-seventeenth century to the late eighteenth century, these individuals held semi-official roles in law, education and religion in the small colonial villages of New Netherland and later Dutch settlements.

The duties of a voorlezer were not just diverse but also essential. Often serving as assistants to pastors, they played crucial roles in religious services, where they would read scriptures and lead congregations in prayer. Without

Van Pelt Avenue, Mariners Harbor. *NYPL Digital Collection.*

a pastor, a voorlezer would step up to conduct religious ceremonies and provide spiritual guidance to the community, underscoring their integral role in the community. However, their contributions were not limited to the church. A voorlezer might also take charge of education, running schools and teaching children basic literacy and religious principles. In this way, they were instrumental in shaping the spiritual and their society's intellectual and moral fabric. Over the centuries, the Voorlezer's House has served as a private residence, storefront and lunch counter. However, in 1939, the Staten Island Historical Society restored it. The building is now a National Historic Landmark and is recognized as the oldest schoolhouse in the United States. It has been carefully arranged to resemble the eighteenth-century schoolhouse where the schoolmaster lived when school wasn't in session. The home's sole inhabitant to hold the title of voorlezer, Hendrick Kroesen, resided on the property only from 1696 to 1701. Subsequently, the present structure served as a private residence for over a century. Today, it is owned and operated by the Staten Island Historical Society.

The Parsonage
Arthur Kill Road and Clarke Avenue

The Parsonage, built in 1855, stands at its original location on Arthur Kill Road and Clarke Avenue. It served as the residence for pastors of the now-demolished Dutch Reformed church. This Carpenter Gothic–style building features intricate exterior woodwork, known as gingerbread details, and retains many of its original interior elements. It remains a notable example of Gothic Revival architecture, with two stories and a one-story porch wrapping around two sides.

The Dutch Reformed church established a presence on the corner of Center Street and Arthur Kill Road in 1769, succeeding the Voorlezer's House. Though the original church was destroyed by the British in 1776, a new church was erected in 1808. In the 1850s, as the congregation sought a full-time pastor, a committee including H.B. Cropsey and Richard Tysen oversaw the construction of the Parsonage. Over the next two decades, it housed four successive ministers of the South Reformed Dutch Church, with a kitchen extension added during this period.

The South Reformed Dutch Church's Parsonage has a rich history of occupants. Reverend Thomas Ruggles Gold Peck, the Parsonage's first resident pastor, was known for his energetic demeanor. Following his departure, subsequent ministers and their families resided there, including Reverend Erskine N. White and Reverend Jacob Fehrman. By 1875, financial struggles led to the church renting the Parsonage to private individuals, like Ann Guyon Mundy. The church eventually disbanded in 1878, and by the mid-1880s, the building was sold. In 1886, Leah and William L. Flake acquired the property, making various modifications over the years. The Flake family later leased the Parsonage to Dr. Henry G. Steinmeyer, who continued to reside there even after the home was sold to the City of New York in 1953. Subsequent caretakers and temporary uses of the house, including housing administrative offices and a restaurant, followed. Despite these changes, the Parsonage remained a significant landmark, earning an official New York City landmark designation in 1969.

The Parsonage has been the setting for intriguing paranormal experiences. Former guests of the Parsonage Restaurant have shared tales of a lady, seemingly from another era, seen wearing a bonnet and nineteenth-century clothing. The dining room, a stage for the apparitions of soldiers during the day and earlier parts of the night, has witnessed these ethereal figures crossing the building, their destinations seemingly in the nearby cemetery.

When passing by the restaurant late at night, between 10:00 p.m. and 2:00 a.m., many have reported seeing an apparition. This ghostly figure, a woman in old-fashioned clothing and a bonnet, has been spotted in a window on the Parsonage's second floor. On some days, the authenticity of these experiences is further validated by the flickering and swaying of a single light bulb that hangs from the Parsonage's ceiling.

In 2006, the *SCARED* crew returned to Staten Island to investigate the Parsonage Restaurant in historic Richmond Town. Since the Parsonage has long been rumored to be one of the islands' legitimate hauntings, the crew covered the place from top to bottom in detection equipment and brought in a little extra psychic help. *SCARED* conducted an overnight investigation in the Parsonage Restaurant. An investigative team, including a psychic, spent the evening in the restaurant. It was disclosed that a cemetery once sat on the church grounds and that in 1885, twenty-three bodies were exhumed from the site and were relocated to the Moravian cemetery. The investigators believed that although the remains no longer inhabited the area, the spirits may have lingered. The crew talked to the staff, who said they had experienced seeing silverware fly across the room and the signs of a possible poltergeist (a spirit that makes noise or plays pranks, often thought to center on specific individuals, such as a teenager; poltergeists are perhaps not ghosts at all but rather a form of latent telekinetic ability).

The employees also claimed they'd heard footsteps over the bar area and seen glasses break inexplicably.

The team saturated the building with detection equipment and monitored it all evening. A psychic was also brought in, and after prayers were said, sage was used as a cleanser, as it is believed to make spirits move. A female spirit came to the psychic. The spirit's name was Gretchen, and she was a thirty-two-year-old woman who had died of polio. The psychic also sensed the spirits of little girls in the basement and said Hazel, another woman, aged forty, was a happy-go-lucky spirit who liked being in the building.

Throughout the investigation, the team experienced cold spots and some angry spirit energy in the attic. The cold spots could be seen through their breathing and felt on their skin. After the team turned off lights in certain rooms, they would return to find them turned on again. Using EVPs (electronic voice phenomena, which capture and record disembodied voices and sounds), they listened for disembodied voices but were unable to detect any. However, while using the EMF detector (electromagnetic fields, or electromagnetic frequencies, a combination of electrical and magnetic fields, are commonly measured as part of the ghost-hunting process, as some theories suggest that paranormal activity can disrupt or create these fields), they detected spike movements, proving that activity was going on in the Parsonage Restaurant. A recording of their investigation can be seen on Brian Cano's YouTube channel. In 2006, the episode of the *SCARED* cable TV series that was filmed at the Parsonage Restaurant appeared in the inaugural Staten Island Film Festival.

THE BARD AND HENDESON AVENUE GHOST

If the Space Beings want to contact you, they will do so. They do the choosing.
—*Brad Steiger*

Bard Avenue, named after Staten Island businessman William Bard, was laid out by Patrick Hart, a prominent taxpayer in Castleton. Notable figures such as General Richard Delafield, Robert Gould Shaw, Commodore William T. Garner and Dr. Samuel MacKenzie Elliott owned property along this street. The area also housed the Staten Island Cricket Club, a prominent amateur sports club. At the intersection of Bard and Henderson Avenues stood the former residence of George William Curtis, a distinguished Staten Island resident. Curtis successfully advocated for preserving a majestic elm tree by influencing the rerouting of Henderson Avenue.

Staten Islanders are likely familiar with Curtis High School, named after George William Curtis, a figure known for his activism against slavery, advocacy for women's suffrage and commitment to political honesty. His legacy extends to landmarks like Curtis Avenue, Curtis Court and Curtis Place.

Hans Holzer was a paranormal investigator who traveled worldwide to investigate haunted houses. In his book *Yankee Ghosts*, he recounted an investigation in which he singled out a spirit from a Victorian residence on a gently curved avenue in Staten Island, Henderson Avenue, in 1966. During the investigation, Holzer spoke with a young female psychic who had noticed odd activities in a relative's house. The woman was very sensitive to such things and was concerned about the troubled spirit wreaking havoc on the property.

Hans Holzer was an Austrian-born author who became interested in the paranormal at a young age and wrote over 140 books on supernatural phenomena ranging from ghosts, the afterlife and witchcraft to extraterrestrial beings. He completed his higher education at the University of Vienna. However, he immigrated to New York in 1938, just before the Nazi takeover of Austria. Despite facing several challenges, he pursued his passion for exploring the paranormal world and became a well-known figure in supernatural research. Mr. Holzer called himself "a scientific investigator of the paranormal." He disliked the word *supernatural*, since it implied these phenomena were beyond the reach of science. He did not believe in the word *belief*, which suggests an irrational adherence to ideas not supported by fact. Nevertheless, he was deeply fascinated with the paranormal and dedicated his life to researching and understanding it.

Carolyn Westbo, the niece of the owner of the troubled house, possessed a psychic ability that many people believe is a natural ability we all have, which can lie dormant and be awakened and developed. While Carolyn was in her aunt's house, she often felt anxious and depressed and had an overwhelming need to wring her hands. Her aunt had frequently observed vapors in the home, especially when alone, but she claimed to feel comforted by their presence. She also experienced poltergeists in the house. One day, while Carolyn was there, a mist appeared and became a nebulous female form. The filmy presence distinctly wrung its hands.

Like most poltergeists, the Henderson Avenue spirit liked to steal things off the table, especially baked pies. The trickster pilfered silver spoons and kept them in unusual places, like the bedroom chest of drawers.

Bard Avenue looking south from its intersection with Henderson Avenue, West Brighton. *NYPL Digital Collection.*

During his investigation, Holzer partnered with renowned medium Sybil Leek. Sybil Leek proclaimed herself a witch and wrote and lectured widely on the occult, mystical and supernatural. Mrs. Leek, a native of England, once described herself in an interview as "just an ordinary witch from the New Forest in England" and said her family had been involved in witchcraft since 1134.

While in a trance, Sybil connected with the spirit of a previous resident and perceived her handwringing. The woman's distress resulted from her inability to enter the house. She needed to take care of her family. She felt extreme pain and was unable to ascend the front steps. Sybil sensed the woman had suffered a heart attack outside the home and died instantly, although her death had occurred ten years earlier. The haunting remained earthbound, as she was unaware of her death.

Sybil went on to gently inform the woman of her death and encouraged her to move on to where her loved ones were waiting for her on the other side. Fortunately, after that, the haunting activity purportedly ended.

69 DELAFIELD PLACE

The answer, my friend, is blowin' in the wind.
The answer is blowin' in the wind.
—*"Blowin' in the Wind," Bob Dylan*

Staten Island has been home to many interesting people throughout history, including Dr. Samuel Mackenzie Elliott, an ophthalmologist who had practices in both Manhattan and Staten Island. During the Civil War, he served as an abolitionist, lieutenant colonel and brigadier general (by brevet). Dr. Elliott was not just a pioneer in several surgical procedures, including cataract removal, but he was also a trailblazer in the field of ophthalmology. He graduated from the College of Surgeons in Glasgow, Scotland, in 1828. He then investigated the eye's anatomy and climate's effects on it. Although the term *oculist* was not widely used then, it was what Dr. Elliott preferred to call himself. He had completed the usual medical and surgical training but was determined to specialize in treating eye diseases. He studied the laws of light and the influence of the atmosphere on it. He made microscopic observations of insects, reptiles, fish, birds and quadrupeds, leaving a lasting impact on the field of ophthalmology.

Samuel Mackenzie Elliott, born in 1811, emigrated from Scotland to the United States in 1833. By 1836, newspaper advertisements for his Manhattan practice had surfaced after his arrival on Staten Island. Operating from 11:00 a.m. to 4:00 p.m., Elliott offered free consultations at his Broadway office (located at Duane Street) for those unable to afford his services. An enterprising individual, Elliott later extended his hours until 6:00 p.m. and marketed a patented eye medicine that was said to cure eye inflammation for the modest price of fifty cents, complete with a warranty. Around 1845, he formulated an ointment designed to rejuvenate and maintain hair, which he distributed without charge. Such was his renown that by the early 1840s, oculists who had apprenticed under his guidance proudly proclaimed their affiliation with him in advertisements published in New York newspapers.

Dr. Elliott's unconventional eye surgery method was one of his most interesting practices. Before anesthetics and painkillers, he would have his patients lie on the floor and secure their heads between his knees to perform eye surgeries. Despite his unorthodox approaches, Elliott was adored and respected for his effectiveness. His office was a magnet for patients seeking consultation and treatment, drawn by his reputation for delivering results. So remarkable was his success that scores of notable individuals sought appointments with him and invested in properties near his Staten Island office.

Henry Wadsworth Longfellow; Sidney Howard Gay, an eminent attorney, journalist and abolitionist in New York City; General Winfield Scott, celebrated for his valor in the Mexican War; and Mrs. Sarah Shaw, the spouse of Francis G. Shaw and mother to Colonel Robert Gould Shaw, all sought treatment from Elliot. Such was the doctor's influence that Livingston was affectionately called Elliottville.

Elliott's passion for astronomy led him to establish an observatory at one of his residences on Serpentine Road, now known as Howard Avenue, on Grymes Hill. His property portfolio extended to Bard Avenue, Shore Road (currently Richmond Terrace) and various locations throughout West Brighton. Elliott meticulously inspected each house he constructed, reportedly residing in each, to identify any flaws. It's speculated that he designed twenty-two distinct residences on the island. According to later accounts, Elliott's own residence and several of his cottages purportedly served as shelters for runaway enslaved people who were navigating the Underground Railroad. His home's basement fireplace and apartment were utilized for this cause. Situated across from Walker Park, Delafield Place now hosts the Dr. Samuel MacKenzie Elliott House. The Landmark Preservation Commission recognizes it as an outstanding specimen of country Gothic Revival architecture. Crafted from locally quarried random stone, this edifice's robust appearance dates to around 1840, and its walls are an impressive twenty-three inches thick.

During the Civil War, Elliott's dedication to his country was unwavering. He earned the title of colonel in the Seventy-Ninth Regiment and was a fearless leader. However, his military career was abruptly halted during the First Battle of Bull Run when his horse was shot, causing him severe spinal injuries. Undeterred, Elliott's fervent convictions led him to form the Highland Brigade. Leveraging his Scottish heritage, he placed newspaper advertisements seeking "red-headed Macs with a bad temper" to bolster the ranks of the Seventy-Ninth Highlanders. His daughter, Elizabeth, assumed the role of enrolling officer, while all three of his sons, who had received medical education under his tutelage, enlisted in the brigade. By the war's conclusion, Elliott was bestowed with the commission of brigadier general.

According to Staten Island historian Pat Salmon, Dr. Elliott, alongside his wife and esteemed neighbors Francis and Sarah Shaw, embarked on a chilling séance within the confines of his home. They conducted the séance to investigate mysterious rapping noises they experienced in their home. They devised a method for the spirit to reveal its identity: a single tap for the letter

A, a double tap for B and so forth. To their horror, the spirit communicated a name enveloped in consonants. Dr. Elliott discerned it to be his Welsh grandmother lingering within the shadows of the abode.

Yet amid the unsettling atmosphere of 69 Delafield Place, the spectral visitation of Dr. Elliott's ancestral kin was not the most harrowing incident to unfold within the walls of his medical practice. For now, Dr. Elliott lies in eternal repose in Silver Mount Cemetery in Staten Island, leaving tales of unearthly encounters and frightening procedures that continue to resonate through the ages.

PETTICOAT LANE

May your pockets be heavy and your heart be light.
May good luck pursue you each morning and night.
—Irish blessing

Robbins Corner marks the intersection of Richmond Road and Rocklands Avenue, the latter once known as Petticoat Lane. Named after Nathaniel Robbins, a resident during the Revolution, this junction holds a piece of Staten Island's intriguing history. In the heart of what is now New Springville, along what we know today as Rockland Avenue, lies a tale of mystery and the supernatural, as recounted by Staten Island historian Patricia Salmon. In the mid-nineteenth century, before Rockland Avenue earned its current name, it was referred to as New Road, a rugged path scattered with boulders and tree stumps that dissuaded travelers and settlers alike. Amid this rustic landscape stood a peculiar structure that was partly nestled in the earth and constructed from stones and logs. This arcane dwelling was the home of Hank Vandeveer and his daughter, Nauchie, the latter of whom developed an eccentric reputation.

Known as Schelm Hank, *schelm* being the German word for "rascal" or "scoundrel," Hank harbored a fear of witches, evident from the four horseshoes he affixed to his dwelling's entrance to ward off supernatural forces. Horseshoes, steeped in folklore, symbolize protection and good luck, a tradition dating back to the Middle Ages, when they were believed to repel witches and evil spirits.

Hank and Nauchie were reclusive figures who rarely ventured into the outside world. Nauchie, adorned in eleven-layered petticoats, notably wore an outer layer that was a dingy, dirty blue. In the social norms of the 1860s,

Above: Horseshoes, folklore symbols believed to ward off misfortune, adorn homes worldwide. *Library of Congress.*

Left: Old-fashioned advertisements for petticoats. *NYPL Digital Collection.*

adherence to propriety and modesty was paramount. Yet Nauchie's eccentric behavior set her apart.

Following Hank's passing, Nauchie withdrew further from society, keeping her outer blue petticoat draped around her lower body. Upon Nauchie's demise, she was laid to rest beside her father. However, sightings of her haunting petticoat persisted within the community of New Springville. A spectral presence, the dirty blue petticoat appeared to wander the moonlit nights, earning the road the ominous moniker Petticoat Lane. The spiritualist movement of the era, with its belief in communicating with the deceased, added an eerie dimension to the tale. Yet the climax occurred in 1862, when lightning struck the petticoat and Hank's house, ending the piece of clothing's spectral wanderings. With the demise of the roaming petticoat, humans could finally traverse old Hank's property, marking the resolution of a haunting chapter in New Springville's history.

SHIPYARDS

Give me a job, give me security,
Give me a chance to survive.
—*"Blue Collar Man (Long Nights)," Styx*

The history of Tottenville is connected to the shipyards that once thrived in the area. These shipyards, like A.C. Brown, Ellis and Rutan, were not just structures but also symbols of a vibrant era. Their names still echo at the shores of Ward's Point, reminding us of their historical significance. Located at the southernmost tip of Staten Island, Ward's Point is now part of Conference House Park. There is even a "South Pole" that stands near Ward's Point to mark it as the southernmost site in the state. However, as the twentieth century ended, the shipyards slowly faded into obscurity, their wooden remains creaking with the weight of forgotten dreams. Yet their memories lie dormant beneath the tranquil waters, waiting for the call of war to awaken them again.

In pre-colonial times, Ward's Point and the area that is now known as Conference House Park were favorite spots for the Native Lenape people. The convergence of the Raritan and Arthur Kill Rivers, where they empty into the shallow opening of Raritan Bay, creates an inviting habitat for oysters and clams. The Lenape took full advantage of these mollusks as a food source and built temporary villages near the shore during the summer and fall. Farther inland, deer, turkeys, heath hens and other game animals provided the Natives meat sources. As the centuries passed, the use of this area evolved significantly. During World War I, Tottenville's shipyards played a crucial role in the war effort.

The demand for ships surged, and these shipyards, including the Cossey Shipyard, emerged from the depths of history. Their legacy lives on in the souls of their 1,149 vessels that sailed into the unknown, serving their country in the war. Today, amid the tranquil expanse of Arthur Kill Road and Bentley Street, the spirits of the past still wander. One powerful panic created a terrible fear among the shipyards' employees, according to a *New York Times* article published on October 1, 1907. Two watertight concussion bombs, containing enough powder to blow up an ocean steamship, were found floating in the water off Sanford Ross's drydock at Clifton, causing a panic among the seventy-five men who were at work in the shipyard, and it was several hours before the excitement quieted down. The drydock adjoined the Baltimore and Ohio Railroad's repair shops. But it wasn't

A.C. Brown and Sons Shipyard, Tottenville. *NYPL Digital Collection.*

The Staten Island Ship Building Company's plant, Mariners Harbor. *NYPL Digital Collection.*

believed the bombs were put in the water with the purpose of blowing up either structure.

The mysterious bombs were fished out of the water and dropped onto the drydock as the workers ran for their lives. When the expected explosion failed to materialize, the yardmaster, the bookkeeper and a workman picked the bombs up and brought them to the Stapleton Police Station. The bombs were then soaked for an hour and opened. The two bottle-shaped bombs were identical, both twelve inches long and three inches thick. Each contained five tubelike compartments filled with powder, according to the *New York Times* article, leaving many unanswered questions.

Bethlehem Steel

Bethlehem Steel's shipyard in Staten Island began in the McWilliams Repair Yard in Jersey City, New Jersey, where William Burlee had been a superintendent. Burlee started this yard in Port Richmond in 1888, changing its name to Burlee Dry Dock after McWilliams retired in 1895. In 1898, he took over the neighboring Port Richmond Iron Works and started building engines and steel and wooden vessels. In 1903, he expanded again to Mariners Harbor, and in 1907, its name was changed again to Staten Island Shipbuilding (SISB). In 1929, SISB merged with five other yards in New York Harbor: Theodore A. Crane's Sons Co., James Shewan and Sons, W.&A. Fletcher and Co., Morse Dry Dock and Repair Co. and New York Harbor Dry Dock Co. The new organization was called United Dry Docks, later changed to United Shipyards. In the new structure, most barges and small vessels were built in Crane's yard in Brooklyn, and the larger ships were built in Mariners Harbor. Bethlehem Steel bought the company in June 1938 and expanded its capabilities for World War II with the aid of $6 million from the navy. After the war, the small yards were closed, and the Mariners Harbor yard reverted to building tugs and barges before closing in 1959. This shipyard produced many ships during World War II that helped the United States win the war, and it employed hundreds of Staten Islanders as shipbuilders. Though the shipyards have faded into oblivion, their legacy persists in the memories of those who were fundamental to the industry. Their spectral presence haunts those who dare to remember and reminds us of the men and women who worked there and their contributions to our nation's history.

4
HOSPITALS AND INSTITUTIONS

SEAVIEW HOSPITAL AND NEW YORK FARM COLONY
BRIELLE AVENUE

I'm not crazy; I'm just a little unwell.
I'm not crazy; I'm just a little impaired.
— "Unwell," Matchbox Twenty

Seaview Hospital, located on Brielle Avenue in Willowbrook, Staten Island, New York, is significant in the borough's history. Its haunting past stretches back to its origins as the Richmond County Poor Farm in 1829. Later known as the New York City Farm Colony, it merged with Seaview Hospital in 1915, gaining recognition for its groundbreaking treatment of tuberculosis. This included using fresh air, sunlight and a balanced diet, which were innovative approaches at the time and contributed to the hospital's pioneering efforts in healthcare.

One former staff member, Linda D., served for twenty-five years at Seaview Hospital, initially as a food service director and later as an associate director of adult day health care services. She recounted eerie experiences had there, like a security guard claiming to hear a children's chorus singing Christmas carols, only to discover there once was a children's ward choir at the hospital. Another chilling tale involved a grandmother's claim that her grandchild saw children in the trees behind the ward. These spirits beind the ward are often seen by children.

Seaview Hospital served as a sanctuary for tuberculosis patients, leading to multiple medical innovations. *NYPL Digital Collection.*

According to *Psychology Today*'s Frank T. McAndrew, PhD ("Why Some People See Ghosts But Others Never Do"), humans may be evolutionarily predisposed to seeing ghosts and other paranormal entities. If you've seen one, you're among 18 percent of Americans who have had this experience. While anyone might see a ghost under the right conditions, some people are more prone to these encounters.

Reports of paranormal activity abound, with staff feeling sudden rushes of energy and a sense of being surrounded by spirits. The hospital's history is steeped in the sorrow of lives lost to tuberculosis, with a museum documenting the names and occupations of the hospital's residents during the pandemic. As medicine evolved and societal norms shifted, Seaview Hospital's purpose transformed, leading to its closure in 1975. The site, once an example of healthcare, fell into disuse, becoming a source of urban legends and tragedy, with reports of hauntings and a series of child disappearances.

Despite the hospital's somber past, the community rallied to breathe new life into the area. Several buildings have been rejuvenated to house the new Seaview Hospital Rehabilitation Center and Home and community facilities. The site's historical importance was recognized with its designation as a city landmark and historic district in 1985 and its inclusion in the National Register of Historic Places in 2005.

Metropolitan Life Insurance Representatives

En Route
Dedication of the Tuberculosis Sanitarium for Employees

A MetLife building advertisement. *NYPL Digital Collection.*

Today, the complex stands as a testament to the resilience of Staten Island's history, blending the reverberations of the past with efforts to create a brighter future amid the darkness of its haunting legacy. This transformation is not solely the result of institutional efforts; it is also due to the dedication and commitment of the local community, who recognize the importance of preserving the site's history and transforming it into a space that serves present needs.

It's worth noting that visiting Seaview Hospital can be a bit creepy, especially at night. Stories of paranormal activity and hauntings have contributed to the hospital's reputation as a spooky place. However, despite the hospital's eerie past, it's important to remember its significant role in Staten Island's history and healthcare's evolution.

WAGNER COLLEGE, CUNARD HALL
631 HOWARD AVENUE

I hurt myself today to see if I still feel.
What have I become, my sweetest friend?
Everyone I know goes away in the end.
—*"Hurt," Johnny Cash (originally by Nine Inch Nails)*

This magnificent Italianate villa stands amid the green landscape of the Wagner College campus, a testament to the grandeur of a bygone era. Cunard Hall is a timeless masterpiece that dates to 1852, when it was lovingly crafted as the abode of Mary Cunard and her esteemed husband, the illustrious shipping magnate Edward Cunard. Adorned with intricate architectural details and surrounded by lush gardens, this stately residence exudes an aura of elegance, refinement and paranormal activity. As the years passed, Cunard Hall witnessed the ebb and flow of history, each chapter infusing it with stories and legends. Following the passing of its esteemed occupants, the estate underwent a transformation, becoming a well-known summer retreat. Laughter and joy filled its halls. The property became the Hotel Bellevue, a summer resort colony established in the 1890s on the former Cunard estate. The thirty-eight-acre tract had a great view overlooking the Verrazanno Narrows, New York Harbor and the open sea. It also had several good, usable buildings and plenty of space for more.

Yet with these good times came the whispers of a haunting tale, which created a mystery around Cunard Hall. In the annals of the Halloween 2002

Wagner College, Grymes Hill. *NYPL Digital Collection.*

issue of the *Wagnerian,* a tale emerged—a tale often repeated but always ambiguous. Legend has it that the memories of a tragic event from 1890 linger within these walls, as an unfortunate soul met their demise after leaping from a second-story window. Though no concrete evidence supports this story, the whispers persist, casting intrigue over the grandeur of Cunard Hall. Students report seeing the spirit of the deceased man and hearing the voice of a disembodied woman.

The allure of the unknown continues to captivate the imagination of those who dare to tread Cunard Hall's hallowed grounds.

SAINT JOHN'S UNIVERSITY, FLYNN HALL
300 HOWARD AVENUE

And the three men I admire most
The Father, Son, and Holy Ghost
They caught the last train for the coast.
—"American Pie," Don McLean

Perched majestically on Grymes Hill, the grand edifice known as Flynn Hall is a testament to a bygone era, its Georgian-style architecture exuding timeless elegance and grace. The home was originally constructed in the early twentieth century as part of the illustrious Gans family estate, a sprawling 16.5-acre property that boasts a rich history steeped in maritime lore, mirroring the family's esteemed shipping empire. Settled amid the lush greenery of Staten Island, Flynn Hall commands breathtaking views of the New York Harbor, a picturesque backdrop befitting its storied past. Once embraced by St. John's University, Flynn Hall served as a beacon of knowledge and enlightenment, its hallowed halls echoing with the laughter of students and the wisdom of scholars. Yet beneath its façade of scholarly pursuits lies a realm shrouded in mystery and intrigue, as tales of spectral visitors have long haunted its corridors.

Whispers of the mansion's former occupants, their ethereal presence lingering long after the sun sets, weave a tapestry of ghostly lore that captivates the imagination of all who dare to tread its hallowed grounds. Students, maintenance staff and campus security officers alike have told tales of inexplicable phenomena, from phantom footsteps echoing through deserted hallways to hushed whispers that linger in the stillness of the night.

Among the countless encounters with the supernatural, one tale stands out, etched into the annals of Flynn Hall's haunted history. While going about his nightly rounds, a campus safety officer was drawn to the former butler's pantry by faint noises and the unmistakable scent of cigar smoke wafting through the air. With trepidation, he ventured into the dimly lit chamber, only to be met with the eerie sight of a shadowy figure looming in the corner, adorned with a thick mustache and spectacles. Yet as swiftly as the apparition appeared, it vanished into the ether, leaving behind naught but a lingering chill in its wake.

Now, with St. John's University's departure, Flynn Hall stands silent and still, its halls bereft of the bustling energy of academia. Yet as night falls and darkness descends on Grymes Hill, one cannot help but wonder: Who will the mansion's resident ghosts visit now as they wander the ethereal realms between the past and the present? Only time will tell, as Flynn Hall's enigmatic legacy continues to unfold, a testament to the enduring allure of the unknown.

WILLOWBROOK STATE SCHOOL
CURRENTLY THE COLLEGE OF STATEN ISLAND

Courage is not the absence of fear, but the triumph over it.
—Long Walk to Freedom, *Nelson Mandela*

Willowbrook State School, a significant establishment founded in 1948, was created for individuals with developmental disabilities. It was the largest institution of its kind in the world and aimed to segregate the disabled from society. During World War II, the facility was repurposed as Halloran Hospital, serving as a medical center and a prisoner of war camp until 1951. Halloran General, the 382-acre campus that became a U.S. Army debarkation hospital in World War II, was created by the State of New York. As the school's construction was nearing completion, the army took over the facility in September 1942. It was modified with the addition of numerous facilities, including a surgery wing; 3.5 miles of covered, heated walkways to connect all the buildings; a Red Cross auditorium that could seat 1,200; and labs for fabricating artificial eyes and limbs. The hospital's vast food services complex could prepare as many as 93,000 meals per month, and its sophisticated telephone system included jacks at patients' beds. The hospital also had its own radio station. With a capacity of 1,500 beds, the hospital was activated as an army post on October 19, 1942. Halloran received its first wounded on November 5, 1942. Soon afterward, the decision was made to double its capacity to 3,000 beds, making the facility one of the largest receiving hospitals in the United States. An additional 3,500 beds were stockpiled, and capacity was reserved for the hospital should an emergency or disaster make it necessary. As a debarkation hospital, Halloran gave personnel wounded overseas preliminary care and classified them for transfer to other army hospitals that either specialized in the type of care they needed or were simply closer to their hometowns. The hospital also treated soldiers from the Second Service Command (from New York, New Jersey and Delaware) for injuries and illnesses that local station hospitals could not adequately care for. The hospital regularly processed 2,500 patients per day.

One can only imagine the strong emotional energy that might linger in such an environment—the fear, sadness and grief. Despite the fact that the hospital became known for developing innovative techniques for physical therapy, occupational therapy and studies on penicillin and streptomycin, it was destined to be shut down. The political battle to keep Halloran open as a Veterans Affairs hospital failed due to the insistence of the State of New

Halloran General Military Hospital, Willowbrook. *NYPL Digital Collection.*

York that the campus be returned to its original purpose. On March 16, 1950, the VA announced the closure of Halloran.

Following the hospital's closure, the site reverted to its initial function as Willowbrook State School. The site's history is a testament to the resilience of the school's students and their families, who endured mistreatment and neglect. Despite their grim reality, they held onto hope. The lack of sufficient staff and the dire conditions caused by budget cuts were further exacerbated by overcrowding and inadequate supervision. Families faced a difficult choice in placing their children in impersonal institutions like Willowbrook, hoping for better care and opportunities. Senator Robert F. Kennedy's visit in 1965 famously labeled Willowbrook as "a snake pit," a stark reminder of its descent into inhumanity. In 1972, Willowbrook physicians and ABC reporter Geraldo Rivera collaborated to expose the dire conditions at the facility. This televised investigation gave Willowbrook's residents and families a voice, leading to a groundbreaking 1972 class-action lawsuit establishing their constitutional right to protection from harm.

In 1975, a consent judgment from a lawsuit mandated better treatment and services at Willowbrook. This led to the institution's closure in 1987 and a transition to community-based care. By 1981, the number of residents at the facility had been significantly reduced from 6,000 to 250. These revolutionary changes led to the placement of people with developmental disabilities in community residences, the growth of voluntary agencies, the expansion of special education and day programs and the training of various professionals. Although the school's buildings have been demolished, some people claim the area still holds residual energy and hauntings associated with the school due to its dark history of patient mistreatment and neglect.

Decades after the closure of Willowbrook State School, the former campus underwent a significant transformation. It became the site of the College of Staten Island, operated by the City University of New York (CUNY), which opened its doors in 1993. This transition was not just a change of name and purpose but also a reflection of the evolving societal attitudes toward the care and education of individuals with developmental disabilities. In 2016, the College of Staten Island, thanks to the efforts of the Staten Island Developmental Disabilities Council, opened the Willowbrook Mile. This trail winds throughout the campus and has plaques denoting where the wards of the institution once stood. It also has plaques indicating the buildings from the Willowbrook campus that are still standing.

The potential ghosts of Willowbrook hold a significant place in the area's cultural beliefs, representing the persistence of the souls or spirits of deceased individuals.

SAINT GEORGE THEATRE
35 HYATT STREET

Well, someone tell me, when is it my turn?
Don't I get a dream for myself?
Starting now it's gonna be my turn.
—*"Rose's Turn," from* Gypsy

Amid the ongoing renovations and considerations for renovation of New York City's grandest theaters, it's truly a sight to behold a magnificent silver-screen palace like the St. George Theatre, fully restored and once again weaving its magic in the heart of Staten Island. The St. George Theatre, a masterpiece of Eugene DeRosa's design, was unveiled in 1929. Its interior, a stunning tribute to Baroque architecture, is a testament to the grandeur of the era. The theater changed hands in 1938, when the Fabian Theater chain purchased it. From then until 1977, it dazzled audiences as a movie palace under that company's management. However, after its Fabian era ended, the venue faced a string of unsuccessful ventures. Various owners tried to breathe new life into the space, experimenting with a roller rink, an antique showroom and even a nightclub, but none of these endeavors found lasting success. In the mid-1990s, a glimmer of hope emerged with an attempt to revive the theater as a performing arts center. The stage briefly hosted several performances, but this revival proved unsustainable, and the owner eventually surrendered to the challenges. Apart from a cameo appearance in the 2003 film *School of Rock*, in which it served as the backdrop for the finale, the theater remained wrapped in darkness for over three decades. In 2004, the late Rosemary Cappozalo and her daughters started a not-for-profit organization to save this historic theater from being torn down. Rosemary, better known as Mrs. Rosemary, is the woman who taught two generations of Staten Island girls to dance and was the driving force behind the revival of St. George, which now serves as an exquisite performance arena. She donated her life savings (over $1 million) to the organization and "saved" the St. George Theatre. The theater was given a magnificent overhaul and now serves as a performing arts center and luxury hall. For a theater with so much history, the St. George is bound to have a ghost story or two. Radio personality Ken Dashow shared one of his experiences that occurred during a golf outing to benefit the theater. He also recounted the story of his wife, Jane Dashow, who became locked in a bathroom and then released during one of her performances at the theater. No logical explanation was available except that the St. George ghost was pranking patrons again. Other guests have had the same experience in the restroom, and before the door was unlocked, they heard a giggle, perhaps that of a little girl.

Ghost Lights: What Is the Superstition of the Ghost Light?

Time can make you blind.
But I see you now as we're lying in the darkness.
Did I wait too long to turn the lights back on?
—"Turn the Lights Back On," Billy Joel

The ghost light tradition in theaters is surrounded by mystery and superstition, adding an air of intrigue to the sacred halls of these iconic venues. As the final curtain falls and the stage is left in darkness, the solitary glow of the ghost light stands as a light against the shadows, its flickering flame casting an ethereal glow on the empty stage.

Legend has it that the ghost light safeguards against the mischievous spirits who are said to roam the backstage corridors and dressing rooms. By keeping this light burning throughout the night, theater crews hope to ward off any spectral pranksters or disturbances, ensuring the stage remains undisturbed until the next performance. Yet another, more mystical interpretation of the ghost light's purpose exists. Some believe that it serves as a guiding light for the restless spirits that are said to inhabit every theater. These ghostly apparitions, be they the spirits of long-lost actors or lost souls seeking solace, are said to find comfort in the gentle glow of the light, guiding them on their journey through the afterlife. In this way, the ghost light becomes a practical necessity and a symbol of reverence and respect for the spirits within the theater's walls. It is a gesture of acknowledgment, a silent tribute to the stage's rich history and enduring legacy, where the past and present converge.

So, the next time you find yourself in the hushed stillness of a darkened theater, take a moment to appreciate the flickering glow of the ghost light. In its soft illumination lies a tale of superstition, folklore, mystery and magic that continues to captivate the imagination of theater lovers everywhere.

FORT WADSWORTH
210 NEW YORK AVENUE

Wadsworth's hauntings teeter on the unbelievable. They are the types of tales that are creepy enough to read but easy to dismiss because of their sheer improbability. After all, how many people will actually see a glowing apparition in a Civil War uniform marching through one of the former military installation's underground tunnels?

Built around 1636 as a Dutch blockhouse, the fort was fortified by the British in 1779 and used as their prime defensive location for the rest of the Revolutionary War. Troops occupied the fort during the War of 1812 and the Civil War but only stood guard during the latter. The original fort structure, including its weaponry, was replaced between 1847 and 1862 to create a new defense system in the United States. Following the rebuilding of the fort, it was named Fort Richmond. The fort was later renamed Fort Wadsworth in honor of Brevet Major General James Wadsworth, who was mortally wounded at the Battle of the Wilderness during the Civil War.

Now a part of the National Park Service, Fort Wadsworth claimed to be the longest continually manned military base in the United States until

Infantry inspection, Fort Wadsworth. *NYPL Digital Collection.*

its closure in 1994. Visitors have reported seeing a ghostly soldier walking through its walls and through moving vehicles on the grounds, and others have had even stranger experiences. One woman had a particularly vivid vision in which she felt like she had been transported back to wartime in the body of a curly-haired nurse. The woman found herself surrounded by dead and dying soldiers; a man then grabbed her arm and yelled at her to get down just as an enormous explosion went off. After the blast, the woman opened her eyes to find she was back in the present. Other visitors have reported similar—though less detailed—experiences in which they saw wounded soldiers who appeared and vanished in the blink of an eye.

From 1955 to 1960, the Fifty-Second Anti-Aircraft Artillery (AAA) Brigade headquarters were at Fort Wadsworth. This brigade oversaw the Nike missile firing batteries of the New York Defenses during the height of the Cold War. The United States Army Chaplain School occupied most of the property from 1974 to 1979.

Since the Park Service took over the fort, the U.S. Coast Guard, army reserve and the park police have maintained buildings throughout the property. However, Hurricane Sandy damaged the property, and large portions of Fort Wadsworth remain abandoned. The Battery Weed, an abandoned structure that once protected the narrows, is photogenic against the Brooklyn shoreline and Manhattan skyline. Visitors travel to Staten Island for these views and haunted experiences.

Many Fort Wadsworth visitors have seen apparitions of soldiers walking through the decaying walls. Others have seen the same apparitions traveling through moving vehicles on the fort's property. For some who have stared at an open field on the property, fallen soldiers suddenly appeared before their eyes. After blinking in disbelief, the apparitions disappeared.

These allegedly haunted experiences allude to only some of the secrets hidden within the walls of Fort Wadsworth. Before Hurricane Sandy, the public only knew the Endicott Batteries existed within the fort. However, the severe hurricane exposed the entrance to a new battery after a section of a cliff collapsed. What other wonders exist within Fort Wadsworth?

5

CEMETERIES, DOCKS AND PARKS

And I would've liked to know you
But I was just a kid
Your candle burned out long before
Your legend ever did.
—*"Candle in the Wind," Elton John*

At cemeteries, every headstone tells a story. New York City's early history boasted numerous small burial sites. While an 1830 ordinance barred burials south of Canal Street, Staten Island's rural landscape preserved its burial grounds, which evolved into the first community cemeteries. However, neglect and misuse led to many cemeteries falling into disrepair until the Friends of Abandoned Cemeteries of Staten Island (FACSI) took up the cause of repairing them in 1981. Since then, FACSI has tirelessly worked to restore these sacred spaces, reclaiming them from overgrowth and documenting their historical significance.

MORAVIAN CEMETERY AND
THE VANDERBILT FAMILY CEMETERY AND MAUSOLEUM
RICHMOND ROAD

The Moravian Cemetery is a historic graveyard located on Richmond Road in Staten Island. Established in 1740, the cemetery is open to people of all faiths and is the final resting place of many well-known people, including photographer Alice Austen. The Moravian Cemetery holds a chilling reputation for spectral encounters and eerie happenings. Its haunting tales have spread far and wide, drawing in curious visitors eager to experience the supernatural firsthand. Among the reported phenomena are the faint cries of a phantom infant. Yet it's not just auditory apparitions that haunt this sacred ground; sightings of ethereal figures, including the glowing form of a young girl, her hair flowing like mist around her, have been recounted. The mysterious appearance of a gentleman in formal attire, who materializes only to vanish into the night, has also been reported. Such accounts create mystery and intrigue, making the Moravian Cemetery a place where the boundary between the living and the dead seems to blur, inviting daring souls to explore its haunted history. The Vanderbilt Family Cemetery and Mausoleum is a private burial site adjacent to the Moravian Cemetery. It was designed by Richard Morris Hunt and Frederick Law Olmsted in the late nineteenth century, when the Vanderbilts were the wealthiest family in America. The mausoleum houses the remains of prominent William Henry Vanderbilt (1821–1885), an American businessman and philanthropist, and Cornelius Vanderbilt, who was born in Port Richmond, Staten Island, and died in 1877. The American shipping and railroad magnate acquired more than $100 million in personal fortune. Separate from the rest of the cemetery and built right into a hill, the tomb is at least three stories tall and took Richard Morris Hunt over a year to design and build.

A tragic incident occurred at the cemetery when a twenty-four-year-old woman named Patricia lost her life. While visiting the Vanderbilt Family Cemetery and Mausoleum with her sister, she tried to close the fifteen-foot-tall, ornate ironwork gate, which fell on her and crushed her. Despite the efforts of seven men who came to help, Patricia passed away a few hours later at Staten Island Hospital.

As a result, there have been sightings of spectral beings and eerie cries around the mausoleum. Perhaps the most famous things concerning the Vanderbilt tomb are the photographs taken in that area. Many visitors have claimed that once the film was developed, the people who posed in the picture aren't there anymore—and even more disturbing, sometimes extra people appear.

Many pictures have also revealed orbs, bright lights and lines, blurred faces and even floating, disembodied heads. Another famous story says that the ghostly form of a man in a gray suit will chase away anyone who brings flowers. This apparition is believed to be the ghost of Cornelius Vanderbilt himself. Since Patricia's death, the mausoleum has not been accessible to

Left: A portrait of Cornelius Vanderbilt, an industrial tycoon and philanthropist who amassed vast wealth through the shipping industry and railroads. *NYPL Digital Collection*.

Below: Vanderbilt Mausoleum, Moravian Cemetery. *NYPL Digital Collection*.

the public, and the Moravian Cemetery has increased its security due to the amount of trespassing that takes place there. Still, the supposed haunting remains just as active.

BARON HIRSCH CEMETERY
1126 RICHMOND AVENUE

Baron Hirsch Cemetery is a testament to Jewish heritage and history. Spanning approximately eighty acres, this historic burial ground was established in 1899 and was named after the renowned German Jewish philanthropist Maurice de Hirsch. While the cemetery was initially sustained by around 550 burial societies, responsible for selling grave sites within designated sections, the cemetery's maintenance has faced challenges. These societies disbanded over time due to members passing and a lack of interest from younger generations.

Baron Maurice de Hirsch, a financier and philanthropist who set up charitable foundations to promote Jewish education. *NYPL Digital Collection.*

Despite its significance, Baron Hirsch Cemetery has endured antisemitic vandalism, leading to reports of its rundown condition. Collapsed gravestones, which result from deteriorating foundations, pose hazards within the grounds, serving as a reminder of the potential risks even in well-maintained cemeteries.

Notably, the cemetery gained national attention in January 1960, when yellow paint bearing disturbing messages was smeared on eighty-seven headstones. This incident, along with others, prompted President Dwight D. Eisenhower to caution against the spread of bigotry, warning of its destructive potential on freedom and decency.

Tragedy struck the cemetery in a separate event when a two-thousand-pound monument fell on a middle-aged woman, resulting in her unfortunate demise. The incident occurred during maintenance work, highlighting the need for increased safety measures within such environments.

While reports of ghost sightings are absent from the cemetery, local lore suggests the presence of wandering spirits. Residents in nearby neighborhoods claim to have witnessed apparitions meandering through their yards and streets, evoking unease. Despite this, a resolution to address these concerns still needs to be discovered.

ST. ANDREW'S CHURCH, GRAVEYARD AND PARISH HALL
40 OLD MILL ROAD

The Church of St. Andrew, an Episcopal church, graveyard and parish house in Staten Island's Richmond Town, has a rich history dating to 1708. The first church was built between 1712 and 1713 but was severely damaged around 1867. A new church, constructed in the Gothic style, replaced it in 1872. The churchyard has a small cemetery and a pet cemetery in the back. What's truly fascinating are the reported paranormal phenomena experienced by visitors at the church. They've heard disembodied footsteps and voices, witnessed an organ playing by itself, seen pictures fall off the wall for no apparent reason and felt a sense of being watched. Some have even claimed they saw ghosts within the building, adding to the church's mystique and allure.

The Church of St. Andrew, a cornerstone of American history, was founded in 1708 and chartered by Queen Anne in 1713. It played a pivotal role during the new colonies' fight for freedom, serving as a hospital and headquarters for British soldiers. Reverend Richard Charlton, a figure of significant influence, served as the rector of Saint Andrew's during this time. He was the maternal grandfather of Elizabeth Ann Bayley Seton, the first canonized American saint of the Roman Catholic Church. Alongside her grandparents, her father, brother and sister rest in the church cemetery, a testament to their deep-rooted connection to this sacred place. Reverend Samuel Seabury, another notable figure, was called to be the first bishop of the Episcopal church while serving as rector of the Church of St. Andrew from 1777 to 1780, and he left a lasting legacy.

In a testament to its historical and architectural significance, the Church of St. Andrew was honored in 1967 with a designation by the New York City Landmarks Preservation Commission. This recognition highlights the church's importance to the local community and the broader historical and cultural landscape of Staten Island. The church's cultural significance is further enhanced because it is the final resting place of notable figures.

Elizabeth Ann Seton is an American saint who was born in New York City in 1774 and raised in the Episcopal faith. After her husband's death, she converted to Catholicism and founded the Sisters of Charity of St. Joseph's in Emmitsburg, Maryland, in 1809. She laid the foundation for Catholic education in the United States by establishing St. Joseph's Academy and Free School. She was canonized in 1975 by Pope Paul VI, becoming the first native-born American to become a saint. Her legacy includes religious congregations dedicated to serving the needs of people experiencing poverty in North America and beyond.

In the past, paranormal investigators have descended on St. Andrew's Church in Staten Island, setting up an intricate electronic network within its hallowed halls. Based in Staten Island, the Eastern Paranormal Investigation Center (EPIC) returned to the three-hundred-year-old church to delve deeper into the mysterious phenomena they encountered during their initial visit. EPIC recounted their earlier findings, describing eerie sobbing sounds, phantom footsteps and an unsettling sensation of being watched.

Determined to unravel the church's mysteries, the team designed advanced ghost hunting equipment worth over $20,000. Night-vision infrared cameras were strategically positioned throughout the church, capturing every shadow and movement. Natural EM detectors and EMF meters, designed to detect electromagnetic fluctuations associated with paranormal activity, were carefully deployed. An ion emitter believed to aid in the detection of ghostly manifestations was also utilized to saturate the air with ions, purportedly a source of sustenance for spirits.

The investigation commenced with the equipment in place, and the church was plunged into darkness. The team approached their task skeptically and open-mindedly, determined to explore every possibility. They communicated with the spirits using a K2 meter, a remarkable EMF meter

St. Andrew's Church and its graveyard. *NYPL Digital Collection.*

ideal for paranormal research due to its fast sampling of EMF levels, which makes it highly responsive to ghostly attempts to manipulate its EMF field. These manipulations trigger the meter's LED lights to alert ghost hunters to a spiritual presence.

Reports of strange occurrences, including unexplained sounds, eerie sensations and sightings of apparitions, have fueled rumors of supernatural activity within the cemetery grounds. However, these accounts remain anecdotal and subjective, as there is no conclusive evidence to support these claims of hauntings.

The Sons and Daughters of Italy in America, Father Capodanno Lodge No. 212, meets monthly in the church's newly renovated Hemsley Parish Hall. In the past, members have experienced eerie occurrences, such as lights turning on after they've locked up the hall, doors banging and chairs being arranged. After several members' investigations, complete with ghost-detecting equipment and audio devices, it was determined that the paranormal sounds were made by several men who were using the basement as a shelter for the evening. The mystery was solved!

CHERRY LANE CEMETERY: SPEAKING FOR THE DEAD

Nestled among the modernity of 1440 Forest Avenue in Staten Island lies a forgotten burial ground, once known as Cherry Lane Cemetery. Now, beneath the bustling commerce of a shopping plaza, lies the legacy of those who found their eternal rest there. Among them is Benjamin Prine, the last person born into slavery on Staten Island, who passed away at the age of 106. Like countless others interred there, his story is one of resilience and forgotten history.

Despite efforts to erase their memory, the voices of the deceased echo through the concrete and asphalt, demanding recognition and reverence. For descendants of Prine, discovering their ancestor's resting place sparked a journey of remembrance and advocacy.

The desecration of this sacred ground, where everyday life now treads on forgotten graves, is a painful reminder of the erasure of Black American history. Heather Quinlan's documentary *Staten Island Graveyard* seeks to shed light on this forgotten chapter of New York's past, where the dignity of those laid to rest has been trampled by progress. Amid the rubble and neglect, the call to preserve these sites resonates as an act of reclaiming humanity and honoring the legacies of those who came before. Benjamin Prine's story, immortalized in the newspapers of his time, serves as a beacon of remembrance for future generations. In Ruth Ann Hills's words: "Preserving these burial grounds is more than a duty—it's a revolutionary act, reclaiming the voices of the silenced and ensuring that their memory endures. As the community rallies to give voice to the voiceless, the ground upon which they rest becomes sacred once more, a testament to the resilience and dignity of those who were forgotten but never lost."

Benjamin Prine was the last living person on Staten Island to have been born into slavery. He was reportedly 106 years old when he died in 1900. Though overlooked in the afterlife, he was a well-known figure in the nineteenth century. When he died, he received an obituary in the *New York Times* and in newspapers in other states.

According to his obituary in the *New York Times*, Benjamin Prine was born in 1794 as an enslaved person on Staten Island and passed away at the remarkable age of 106. He lived a life of resilience and accomplishment, driving the first stagecoach on the island and, for fifteen years, making daily trips from Long Neck to Richmond. His childhood included playtime with none other than Commodore Vanderbilt and the Vanderbilt siblings. During the War of 1812, he bravely defended the family and property of his owner from English forces. He also contributed to the construction of fortifications on the island during this tumultuous time. Prine delighted in sharing tales of his past, including memories of the Van Pelt House, where cobblestones lined the kitchen floor and a flat stone served as a hearth. Prine was survived by four children and several grandchildren, and his legacy endures through the stories of his bravery and perseverance. His funeral was held on the Wednesday following his death, a testament to a life well-lived and a man deeply cherished by his family. He was buried in Cherry Cemetery.

THE REZEAU–VAN PELT GRAVEYARD
395 CENTER STREET

Deep in the heart of Historic Richmond Town lies the Rezeau–Van Pelt Graveyard, a testament to Staten Island's rich history. Once a vibrant homestead burial ground, it is now a reminder of bygone days. Enclosed by a fence adorned with eerie symbols, this graveyard tells tales of sorrow and lost time. An angel's head greets visitors at its gate, while winged hourglasses remind all who pass that time is fleeting. Draped urns atop the fence posts serve as silent sentinels to the souls resting within.

Among these hallowed grounds lurks a legend as old as the American Revolution—the tragic tale of Pretty Van Pelt. A cherished figure in her village, she found solace in music and the rhythm of a soldier's drum. But fate dealt a cruel hand when illness claimed her life in 1776, and soon after, her drumming soldier met the same fate.

Yet death could not sever their bond entirely. Witnesses have reported spectral sightings near the Rezeau–Van Pelt Graveyard for centuries. Pretty Van Pelt is said to appear, her ethereal form that of a child draped in a gown, her head adorned with a nightcap. Sometimes, she stands in silent vigil, a spectral bridge between worlds. And other times, she dances, as if to the beat of a phantom drum, perhaps that of her soldier.

In Historic Richmond Town, the past lives on, and the spirits of Pretty Van Pelt and her soldier linger, eternally intertwined in a dance of love and loss.

STATEN ISLAND BOAT GRAVEYARD
NEW YORK CITY'S FORGOTTEN SHIP DUMPING GROUND
ARTHUR KILL, WEST SHORE

This is a place where boats go to die, and it is hard to believe that this place is still within the city limits of New York City. The Staten Island Boat Graveyard is a dumping ground for old, wrecked barges, decommissioned ferries and tugboats. Also known as the Witte Marine Scrap Yard, the Arthur Kill Boat Yard and the Tugboat, the graveyard is a marine scrapyard in the Arthur Kill in Rossville, near the Fresh Kills Landfill on the west shore of Staten Island, New York City. A journey to this unique and thrilling site is an experience. It's an eerie place frozen in time that offers a haunting yet captivating glimpse into a bygone era of maritime history with its decaying vessels.

The Staten Island Boat Graveyard is not just a collection of decaying vessels; it's a testament to a rich and mysterious history that dates to the 1930s. Founded by John J. Witte, it was initially a salvage yard, but as time passed, it became a resting place for many vessels, each with its own story. Despite its grim reputation, the graveyard boasts a certain allure, drawing adventurers and historians alike. The site is home to over two hundred vessels, each with its own unique story. Among these relics are the USS *PC-1264*, a World War II submarine chaser that played a crucial role in the war effort, and the *Abram S. Hewitt*, which was instrumental in many rescue

The Staten Island Boat Graveyard, a marine scrapyard located in the Arthur Kill in Rossville, near the Fresh Kills Landfill on the West Shore of Staten Island. *NYPL Digital Collection.*

operations. Now in a state of decay, these vessels offer a poignant reminder of their past glory.

Navigating to the graveyard presents a challenge, as no official entrances or marked trails exist. It's important to note that visiting during low tide allows for closer inspection of the decaying vessels, though caution is advised due to the murky waters. Wear appropriate footwear and be mindful of your surroundings. While the ship graveyard offers a unique glimpse into maritime history, respecting the site's historical significance and avoiding littering is essential. The ship graveyard may captivate with its ghostly presence. Whether you're drawn to the mysteries of the past or the beauty of the present, the Staten Island Boat Graveyard promises an unforgettable journey into the unknown.

FRESH KILLS LANDFILL

Located in the central-western part of Staten Island, along the banks of the Fresh Kills, this landfill in Staten Island was opened in 1947. It was meant to be temporary but grew to become the largest artificial structure in the world during the second half of the twentieth century. At the landfill's peak, over thirteen thousand tons of garbage were added daily, causing it to grow exponentially until it covered twelve square miles with household waste. However, there was hope that the dump would be remade into one of New York's most prominent parks.

The Fresh Kills Landfill was established by Robert Moses, who negotiated with then–borough president Cornelius A. Hall to build it in Staten Island in exchange for overseeing the construction of the West Shore Expressway. Initially intended to be a two-year operation, the landfill became the primary destination for New York City trash due to industrial growth and convenience, operating until its closure in 2001.

In the 1960s, the landfill became terrible, plagued by foul smells, feral creatures and a rat infestation that threatened to take over the entire island. The odor was vile and immediate. It was caused by bacteria that fed off the rotting trash, creating methane. The foul smell that drifted from the dump stemmed from the aromatic and toxic garbage by-products, which latched onto the volatile methane gas molecules.

Residents there may not have understood the science behind trash decomposition, but they certainly understood the stink. Widespread complaints about the odor were logged as early as 1949. Cleverly, birds were brought in to care of the rats, and the landfill was deemed a wild bird sanctuary.

Fresh Kills Park covers 2,200 acres, making it almost three times larger than Central Park. The park is significant because it was developed on the Fresh Kills Landfill site, the largest landfill in the world before its closure in 2001. The landscape has been reengineered with soil and infrastructure, and the park now serves as a place for wildlife, recreation, science, education and art.

The park's interior is currently accessible only during scheduled park programs, which provide early access to learning and exploration opportunities there.

Fresh Kills Park, the largest park under development in New York City in a century, symbolizes renewal, as it is transforming a former landfill into a sustainable landscape. The park integrates landfill infrastructure into its design, emphasizing environmental sustainability and public engagement. After the closure of the Fresh Kills Landfill in 2001, an international design competition led to the creation of a draft master plan by field operators featuring open grasslands, waterways and engineered structures. The park is set to offer diverse recreational, educational and cultural activities, with phased development prioritizing community connections. Ecologically, the park fosters habitat restoration, supports various wildlife and serves as a unique study site for urban ecosystem development. Engineered systems manage landfill by-products while ensuring environmental safety. Connectivity is ensured through a network of paths and recreational waterways, with plans for public road access. New York City Parks oversees the project's phased implementation, prioritizing community engagement and sustainable development.

After the September 11 attacks, then-governor George Pataki reopened Fresh Kills, and workers transported more than 1.8 million tons of debris, some of it found to be toxic, from Ground Zero to the landfill. The Fresh Kills Landfill became the primary site for dumping the wreckage of the Twin Towers. Forensics investigators regularly searched the debris for clues and remains.

While at the site, an NYPD police officer, retired NYPD sergeant Frank Marra, forty-eight, claimed he saw the ghost of a Black woman dressed in white, like a Red Cross worker from the Second World War. He claimed he saw this specter while going through the debris from the World Trade Center attacks at Fresh Kills Landfill in Staten Island between September 2001 and February 2002. The ghost held a tray of sandwiches and always stood more than fifty yards away before vanishing. Mara claims that at first, he thought she was trying to help, being a first responder. He saw her only a few times and always from a distance, more than fifty yards away each time, but he recalled that the apparition looked like a person.

And while these were rare sightings, Marra stashed them away as memories until about a year later, when he spoke to a retired crime scene detective who mentioned the ghost. The detective asked him if he had ever heard stories about the "old Red Cross worker trying to serve sandwiches and coffees out by the sifters," which brought Marra's memories of the woman rushing back.

However, Sergeant Frank Marra was not the only one who saw the specter, who, as a psychic medium explained, could have been a "soul collector" who guided people to the afterlife. Along with the Red Cross worker, cops and volunteers witnessed other things in the landfill, from shadows to large black masses.

In his book *From Landfill to Hallowed Ground*, Marra details his experience searching through the remains of the World Trade Center attacks from September 2001 to February 2002 at Fresh Kills Landfill. In the aftermath of the September 11 attacks, volunteers who worked at the landfill discovered numerous personal items left behind by victims, a poignant reminder of the tragedy and the people who lost their lives that day. Among the items were sentimental belongings of family members and friends. The first responders and volunteers also played a crucial role in helping identify hundreds of people who had lost their lives during the attacks. Over time, the landfill has become a place of reverence and remembrance. It's a solemn site that may hold deep significance for many. It's not uncommon for people to associate sites of great sadness or horror with visitations from spirits, as it can help us find meaning and understanding amid the pain of loss.

6

LAKES AND FIELDS

SILVER LAKE

Silver Lake Park was established in Staten Island around 1904. It was named after the lake that once surrounded the island but that no longer exists, as it was drained in 1913. Instead, the park now features Silver Lake Reservoir, the final stop of the Catskill Water Supply. When the lake existed, it was a popular spot for boating and ice skating and even hosted the National Skating Amateur Championship in 1897. The state assembly eventually acquired the land around the lake and converted it into public space.

Silver Lake is a neighborhood and reservoir located in Staten Island. The north shore park is bounded by Forest Avenue, Victory Boulevard and Clove Road. The original Silver Lake was created at the end of the last ice age and was a spring-fed body of water. The ice ages began 2.4 million years ago and lasted until 11,500 years ago. During this time, the Earth's climate repeatedly changed between very cold periods, during which glaciers covered large parts of the world, and very warm periods, during which many of the glaciers melted. Today, Silver Lake makes up the south basin of the reservoir. It was once known as Fresh Pond, but by the mid-nineteenth century, the name Silver Lake had come into use, and both names were used interchangeably until around 1860. The lake was named after Mark Silver, previously known as Marks Silva, who founded the Hebrew Free Burial Association. The association purchased the land that became Silver Lake Cemetery, which was used for charitable burials. The cemetery is the final resting place of many of the 1911 Triangle Shirtwaist Factory fire victims.

Silver Lake Park, a public park in New York City, offers tree-lined jogging and walking trails, spacious grassy areas for picnics or sunbathing and twin reservoirs vital to the city's water system. However, in 1878, the park became the scene of a gruesome discovery. On September 15 that year, three boys who were tending cattle on the shoreline stumbled upon a partially buried barrel that contained decomposing human remains. These remains were identified as belonging to Annie Reinhardt, the pregnant wife of Edward Reinhardt, a confectioner from Stapleton. Mrs. Reinhardt had been killed on July 19, 1878, when she was eight months pregnant. Reinhardt had cracked her skull, doused her body with chloroform and concealed her remains in a wooden beer barrel with pillowcases, sheets and an old carpet. Newspaper accounts described Mrs. Reinhardt's head as being covered with a gunny sack, her body bound in the fetal position.

In her 2013 book *Murder and Mayhem on Staten Island*, historian Patricia Salmon covered this murder case, one of the most sensational in Staten Island's history. The case was extensively reported by the press at the time. According to Salmon's book, Mrs. Reinhardt (whose maiden name was Degnan) may have been bludgeoned to death while giving birth, making the heinous crime even more horrifying.

During the trial, Reinhardt claimed that his wife was unhappy with him. However, it was later discovered that Reinhardt had been unfaithful to his wife. According to Salmon, Edward Reinhardt denied that Annie was his wife, as he had already married another woman shortly before Annie's disappearance.

Reinhardt was sentenced to execution and was reported to have shared his jail cell with his three cats as he awaited his fate. Strangely, the gallows used for his execution were specially built for him in the courtyard behind the Richmond County Courthouse in Historic Richmond Town.

On January 14, 1881, Edward Reinhardt was executed by hanging. Public executions were seen as entertainment and a boost for local businesses. On the day of Reinhardt's execution, taverns all over Staten Island hired extra staff to meet the demand of the crowds who wanted to see the event. He was later buried at Silver Mount Cemetery near the lake. Reinhardt was the first individual to be hanged on Staten Island since 1780.

According to Pat Salmon, Annie Degnan Reinhardt's murder is among Staten Island's most chilling. Some suspect she was buried alive by her husband, Edward, near Silver Lake. Edward showed no remorse, even at the gallows, where his only concern was for himself.

Members of the Bechtel family, who ran Staten Island's famous brewery in Stapleton, were also buried in the cemetery. According to Salmon's painstaking account of the Reinhardt case, the barrel Edward used to bury Annie Reinhardt in was traced to the Bechtels' brewery.

Two months after Reinhardt's execution, undertaker Daniel Dempsey claimed he saw Reinhardt's ghost by a barrel on Richmond Turnpike, now known as Victory Boulevard.

The Marine Cemetery in Silver Lake has a sorrowful history. It was located where the eighteenth fairway of the Silver Lake Golf Course stands today. According to Staten Island's records, more than seven thousand Irish immigrants who arrived in New York in the 1840s and 1850s were buried in the cemetery. Unfortunately, these immigrants did not get to start their new lives in America. Instead, they were taken to the New York Marine Hospital, also known as "the Quarantine," in Tompkinsville, where they passed away due to diseases such as cholera, typhus, yellow fever and smallpox.

Opened in 1799, the hospital was burned to the ground in 1858 by a riotous mob who were worried about the constant epidemics that plagued the site. Before its destruction, the hospital had processed hundreds of thousands of immigrants, advance records say, and treated up to 9,000 people a year. It's also said that 1,500 people a year died in the hospital.

The New York City Parks Department took title to the land in 1924, which was converted to its current use as a golf course in 1928.

Doubt over the existence of a burial ground on the golf course persisted for years. Still, by 1994, it was confirmed that the land had previously been used to inter those from the quarantine hospital, including thousands who had fled the Great Hunger in Ireland.

There is now a memorial to Irish immigrants from the old New York Marine Hospital, or "the Quarantine," who were buried at the former Marine Cemetery. The plaque details the deaths of these Irish immigrants and is also a potent reminder of Staten Island's long-forgotten history.

MILLER FIELD

Put silver wings on my son's chest;
make him one of America's best;
he'll be a man they'll test one day.
Have him win the Green Beret.
—*"Ballad of the Green Berets," Barry Sadler and Robin Moore*

Miller Field is a former airfield in New Dorp, Staten Island, that was used by the U.S. Army from 1919 to 1969. It's now part of the Gateway National

Recreation Area and features abandoned hangars, a control tower and recreational paths. The site was originally part of the Vanderbilt family farm but was repurposed for aviation use. An archaeological study later revealed remnants of the Vanderbilt buildings, providing insight into the site's history. Today, it's a popular destination for aviation enthusiasts, military history buffs and outdoor recreation enthusiasts.

In January 1920, the Air Service Coast Defense Field at New Dorp was named Miller Field for Captain James E. Miller. Miller was the first American aviator killed in action while serving during World War I.

Some noteworthy flights at Miller Field occurred in the 1920s. In July 1920, the army took commercial photographers to the skies to create aerial photographs and film of the International Cup yacht races. The newspapers were informed and able to obtain images in the field. This method demonstrated both a timely way to produce photographs and a practical use of airplanes by the public. In 1928, Admiral Byrd tested his new plane, a Ford trimotor, the *Floyd Bennett*, at Miller Field. This plane was used for his first trip to Antarctica in December 1928. In the 1960s, Green Beret units used the field as a training camp. This provided both housing and a reserve training area for them.

Sadly, one of the airfield's most memorable occurrences came when it was the site of the TWA Super Constellation crash, which left 134 people dead.

On December 16, 1960, at 10:33 a.m. EST, two planes headed for New York airports crashed into each other in the air. United Airlines Flight 826, a Douglas DC-8 aircraft, which was soaring into Idlewild Airport (now John F. Kennedy International Airport), collided midair with Trans World Airlines Flight 266, a TWA Lockheed L-1049 Super Constellation, which was headed to LaGuardia Airport. The planes landed in Staten Island's Miller Field and Park Slope, Brooklyn. It was considered one of the deadliest plane crashes of its time, and 134 people perished.

The two jet airliners collided about 5,200 feet over Staten Island, New York. The Lockheed crashed near the collision point on the former Miller Army Air Field, while the DC-8 continued to the northeast before crashing in Brooklyn. All 128 persons on board both airliners perished, as did six people who were on the ground. One passenger, an eleven-year-old boy on board the DC-8, did survive the crash, but he died the next day as a consequence of having inhaled the burning jet fuel fumes.

Since that fateful day, Miller's Field has been the site of alleged paranormal activity, with witnesses reporting a range of phantoms believed to be the spirits of deceased airline passengers.

What may have been even more frightening than the deceased passengers' apparitions was the near-fatal catastrophe that occurred in 2019, when a low-flying plane made an emergency landing at Miller Field in New Dorp, shocking youth soccer coaches and players who were minutes away from starting their games.

The aircraft from Somerset, New Jersey, was required to land due to bad weather. According to the NYPD, no injuries were reported. The landing occurred just after 5:30 p.m., as youth soccer teams were beginning to arrive for their nighttime games. Witnesses said there was a coach and a small number of players on the side of the field where the plane landed.

According to an eyewitness, the plane passed New Dorp High School and then suddenly came down like it was landing, so they immediately hauled the kids off the field. The plane landed in the center of the field and rolled. Fortunately, the landing occurred just before the games were set to begin, so the field was less congested. Perhaps some benevolent ghosts led the distraught pilot and soccer teams to safety.

7

FOLKTALES, URBAN LEGENDS, MYTHS AND HOAXES

A lie can travel halfway around the world while the truth puts on its shoes.
—Mark Twain

What is an urban legend? An urban legend is a modern folktale or story circulated within a community or society. It typically involves elements of the extraordinary, mysterious or supernatural and often serves as a cautionary tale for parents and sparks curiosity about the unknown. These stories may be based on a kernel of truth, but they become embellished or distorted over time as they are retold and spread rapidly through social networks, gaining popularity.

CROPSEY

Once upon a time, there existed a chilling urban legend known as Cropsey in the borough of Staten Island, New York City. It was a tale whispered among children, especially at Staten Island campsites, a cautionary narrative told by parents and a spine-tingling yarn shared among siblings. Cropsey, they said, was a murderous fiend, a figure with a hook for a hand who prowled the shadows, preying on unsuspecting youngsters. The legend created a reign of terror, innocent souls swept away to the depths of an abandoned sanatorium's tunnel system nearby. Through these tales, children learned the vital lessons of vigilance and safety, lest they become another tragic chapter in the legend of Cropsey.

For years, the legend remained just that, a story, a ghoul to keep wandering feet tethered to safety. However, in 1987, the nightmare took on a haunting reality. The residents of Staten Island were jolted from their disbelief when the horrifying figure behind the Cropsey myth was unmasked as Andre Rand, a man charged with heinous crimes that mirrored the legend.

The legend of Cropsey had permeated the local culture deeply. It was the stuff of summer campfire tales, inspiring films like *The Burning* in 1981, which drew eerie parallels to the local lore of Staten Island. In this cinematic incarnation, George Cropsey, once a respectable man, spiraled into madness after a cruel prank disfigured him. Armed with an ax, he became the embodiment of fear, stalking and slaying unsuspecting campers in a chilling reflection of the legend. The legend of Cropsey, born from the collective imagination, transcended its origins, imprinting itself onto the psyche of Staten Island and beyond. The cautionary tale reminded Staten Islanders of the thin veil between myth and reality.

However, beneath the guise of myth lay a chilling reality. Cropsey emerged from the shadows as Andre Rand, a name that reflected depravity. His origins are intertwined with the decaying halls of the Willowbrook Institution. Rand was born Frank Rostum Rushan in 1944. His father died when Rand was fourteen. His mother was institutionalized at Pilgrim Psychiatric Center in Brentwood, New York, where he and his sister would visit her as teenagers. Between 1966 and 1968, using the name Frank Bruchette, Rand worked as a custodian, orderly and physical therapy aide at Willowbrook State School, an ominous backdrop to his descent into darkness.

Andre Rand, also known as the "Pied Piper of Staten Island," was convicted of a series of disturbing crimes, including kidnapping, sexual abuse and unlawful imprisonment. His criminal activities spanned from 1969 to 1987 and primarily occurred in New York, particularly Staten Island and the South Bronx.

Once obscured by legend, the truth came to light in a courtroom. In 1988, Rand was charged with kidnapping and first-degree murder. His reign of terror, fueled by madness and malevolence, left scars on a community's psyche that time could never fully heal.

However, questions lingered like phantoms at night, even in the face of justice. Were there accomplices and sinister rituals? The chilling truth of Cropsey's reign was a grim reminder of the thin veil between myth and reality, a cautionary tale for generations to come.

THE STATEN ISLAND MONASTERY, AUGUSTINIAN ACADEMY GRYMES HILL CAMPUS

Just across Campus Road from Wagner College's main campus stood the historic St. Augustine's Monastery, formerly the site of the Augustinian Academy, a Catholic boys' high school that welcomed students from 1926 to 1969. The history of the Augustinian Academy dates to the late nineteenth century, when the Fathers of the Augustinian Order were interested in establishing a parish on Staten Island.

After its days as a school concluded, the building found new life as a retreat center before eventually closing its doors for good in 1984. The abandoned structure became a fixation for curious youths, drawn to its air of mystery and decay. It turned into a landmark for those intrigued by tales of hauntings.

Local lore refers to it as the Monastery, and it has sparked countless chilling tales. Surrounded by suburban homes, the site is now covered in overgrown vegetation, with turkey vultures prowling the area. Rumors of bodies buried beneath its floors add to its sinister aura. Visitors have reported hearing ghostly whispers and footsteps, creating a genuinely spine-chilling atmosphere.

The Augustinian Academy on Staten Island, founded on May 30, 1899, in conjunction with the new Roman Catholic parish of Our Lady of Good Counsel by the Augustinian Friars. *NYPL Digital Collection.*

Legend has it that a monk's descent into madness led to a massacre, with bodies hidden in secret sublevels beneath the monastery. Some claim these depths extend thirty floors underground, adding to the mystery and horror of the former site.

In 1993, Wagner College stepped in to save the site from commercial developers. Despite these efforts, the building continued to deteriorate over the years, posing a danger to the community. Finally, in 2006, the decision was made to demolish the aging structure, marking the end of an era and closing the chapter on St. Augustine's Monastery's storied past. Though the physical building may be gone, the memory of the Monastery lives on in the hearts of those who walked its halls and the stories shared by those who dared to explore its ghostly echoes.

BACKSEAT KILLER

As a cautionary tale in Staten Island, the "Killer in the Backseat" continues to be told through the generations, with the only upgrade being an available cell phone to call for help. This chilling legend serves as a stark reminder of the potential dangers we may face, even in seemingly safe environments.

It is the story of a young woman on her way home from work at the Staten Island Mall, a short drive that becomes a tale of survival. A Staten Island college student who was working a late shift during the Christmas rush enters her car, tossing her handbag onto the front seat, tired, anxious and a little leery of traveling alone after 10:00 p.m. She is anxious to arrive safely home, knowing the ride will take another thirty minutes. Her family had recently moved to the Garden State. The New Jersey turnpike stretches before her, but she's not alone. In her rearview mirror, she glimpses the ominous silhouette of another vehicle, its headlights glaring like hostile eyes in the night. With each mile, it draws closer, its presence suffocating, like a predator stalking its prey. The high beams of the vehicle pierce the darkness, blinding and taunting her with their relentless pursuit. Fear clenches her chest as she calls 911, desperation in her voice as she pleads for help and explains her situation. Finally arriving at her destination, she pulls into her driveway, seeking refuge in the sanctuary of her parents' home; the nightmare reaches its crescendo. Behind her, the ominous vehicle halts, its driver revealed in the harsh glow of the police's arrival.

But what they uncover is more horrifying than any fiction. With trembling hands raised in surrender, the driver reveals the truth hidden in the shadows of her own car. A figure lurks in the backseat, a specter of malevolence armed with a knife, gloves and tape. Each flash of the high beams was not an act of aggression but a desperate warning, an attempt to protect the woman who was driving frantically home. In the twisted predator and prey scenario, the high beamer becomes an unlikely hero, his actions a salvation in the darkness. Yet even as the threat is thwarted, the lingering dread remains, a reminder that evil can lurk in the most unsuspecting places. The legend of the "Killer in the Backseat" is a chilling reminder that sometimes, the actual monsters are closer than we dare to imagine.

PHANTOM DOG ON VICTORY BOULEVARD: "BEWARE THE SIGNS"

Dogs have been a common aspect of cultural folklore and mythology for thousands of years. Humans first domesticated dogs tens of thousands of years ago and have lived with them ever since. Many cultures have kept them for hunting, as protectors and as pets, so it's obvious why man's best friend has become such a big part of mythology.

Long before the Revolutionary War, when Staten Island was a sparsely settled land with only a few thousand inhabitants, the land was enveloped by miles of dense woods. These woods, along with the few roads that connected the area's villages, farms, orchards and fields, were believed to be haunted by ghosts, witches and even the devil himself. One of the most notorious haunted places was a crossroads called the Signs, located in the Bull's Head area.

Legend has it that a tavern nearby was once visited by a terrifying figure, a tall, dark, handsome man with fiery eyes who never spoke. He would linger until the festivities ended and then disappear into the night. But the unlucky ones who caught his attention would find themselves followed by this shadowy figure. He would trail them without saying a word. Some believed he was the devil himself, capable of taking the form of a large, black dog. The mere thought of encountering such a being sends shivers down one's spine.

On Victory Boulevard, near Signs Road, a dog of colossal proportions once roamed. Its fur was as black as the night, and its eyes glowed with an otherworldly red hue. The dog's howl, a mournful sound that seemed to pierce the silence, would chill even the bravest souls. The dog's cry echoed through the quiet streets, almost as if calling out to someone. This dog was as large as the thousands of working horses that frequented the area from the 1780s to the late 1800s, when horses were the primary power source for transportation in New York City, moving people and goods in coaches and wagons. Even a few decades ago, numerous stables, where residents and visitors could ride stallions, dotted Staten Island, and some people kept horses in their backyards.

The mysterious dog that roamed the streets was a puzzle. It moved with an eerie grace, almost like it was part of the shadows. Some may have seen it as a guardian of the night, silently watching over everyone. But others suspected it harbored darker intentions, perhaps leading unsuspecting souls astray. No matter what you believe, meeting this spooky dog would leave a lasting impression. Its sheer enormity was enough to strike fear into the hearts of those who encountered it. The dog's demeanor made it a truly terrifying sight.

One brave soul, emboldened by a desire to rid the area of this unearthly canine, decided to take matters into his own hands. Armed with a hefty ax, the man mounted his horse and awaited the inevitable confrontation, undeterred by the dog's menacing nature. As the ghostly hound approached, covered in dark hair and with fiery red eyes, the man swung the ax with all his might, desperate to banish the apparition. The dog seemed invincible, even after being hit by the ax. To the man's dismay, the dog vanished into thin air, leaving the ax uselessly clattering to the ground.

Despite the man's valiant efforts, his actions seemed to have little effect on the ghostly hound. For years to come, sightings of the oversized dog persisted; it disappeared and reappeared at will, as if mocking any attempts to thwart its presence. It remained a haunting and enigmatic figure, a constant reminder of the mysteries that lingered along Victory Boulevard, formerly known as the Richmond Turnpike.

Dogs and wolves hold a significant place in various cultures' myths, folklore and beliefs. They are deeply ingrained in our collective consciousness, symbolizing companionship, protection and love. In folklore, dogs often mirror human social tendencies and are essential in stories of transition and guardianship. Stories of werewolves and shape-shifting dogs, for instance, reflect our shared understanding of human and animal nature, blurring the lines between the two.

THE WITCH OF STATEN ISLAND

What do Polly Bodine, Edgar Allan Poe, P.T. Barnum and a horrific crime have in common? Edgar Allan Poe and P.T. Barnum are connected historically to the lesser-known Polly Bodine, a resident of Staten Island, New York, the rural haven inhabited by ten thousand residents in 1843.

The actual crime involved Polly Bodine, who was charged with the horrifying murders of her brother's wife, Emeline Housman, and their infant daughter on the ominous night of Christmas 1843. The scene that greeted those who entered the Housmans' home was a montage of horror—Emeline's life snuffed out, her skull mutilated and her body set ablaze while the infant Ann Eliza met a similarly violent end.

Emeline's husband, George Housman, a fisherman, was away during the fateful night. During his absences at sea, Polly Bodine, his sister, often extended her companionship to Emeline and Ann Eliza. The family ties appeared genuine, and Polly's friendship with Emeline seemed unmarred.

Yet Emeline's sister-in-law, Polly, emerged as an immediate suspect. In an era of stringent social norms, Polly's life carried a shadow. Estranged from her husband, she returned to her parental abode with her two children, just across the street from the Housmans' residence. Polly's associations also took a scandalous turn when she engaged in a relationship with George Waite, a Manhattan pharmacist.

Polly's reputation and her unfortunate circumstances painted her as a prime suspect. The shadow of her guilt loomed larger when reports surfaced that she was spotted consuming gin on the Tompkinsville Ferry after the gruesome events and had subsequently pawned silverware engraved with Emeline's initials. Suspicion grew that the motive might have been rooted in robbery, casting Polly as a potential perpetrator.

Perhaps the greatest enigma about this crime is the lack of any reasonable motive. Polly and Emeline had always been friendly, the dead woman and her husband had no enemies and the amount of missing household goods hardly explained such a shocking double homicide.

Polly was arrested for the murder after the coroner's inquest, accused of wanting to steal $1,000 George had given Emeline. The money was found in the outhouse where Emeline had hidden it. Polly was jailed with George Waite, her lover. By New Year's Day 1844, Polly's fate was sealed within the confines of Richmond Courthouse.

Even P.T. Barnum, a maestro of spectacle, was drawn to the tale and created a wax tableau of the horrific scene. Polly's legal journey was complicated, and her trial was an extravagant spectacle. Ferries were summoned to accommodate the influx of spectators, and reporters were called in from far away.

In 1844, while in New York, Edgar Allan Poe contributed a series of dispatches titled "The Doings of Gotham" to the *Columbia Spy*. These dispatches illuminate his astute observations on legal proceedings, notably Polly Bodine's case. In the June 18 edition of the *Columbia Spy*, the following was printed:

> *The trial of Polly Bodine will take place at Richmond on Monday next and will, no doubt, excite much interest. This woman may, possibly, escape—for they manage these matters wretchedly in New York....And, moreover, very much of what is rejected as evidence by a court, is the best of evidence to the intellect. For the court, guiding itself by the general principles of evidence,—the recognized and booked principles,—is averse from swerving at particular instances. And this steadfast adherence to principle, with systematic disregard of the conflicting exception, is a sure mode of attaining the maximum of attainable truth, in any long sequence of time. The practice, in mass, is, therefore, philosophical; but it is none the less certain that it engenders, in many extraordinary instances, a vast amount of individual error. I have good reason to believe that it will do public mischief in the coming trial of Polly Bodine.*

Charges of murder and arson were leveled against Polly. A thread quickly emerged, as it became evident that not only were lives extinguished that night, but possessions were also purloined. Silverware etched with the initials "E.H." and a watch were among the stolen items, and a malicious fire had been set to conceal the unspeakable acts.

Polly's initial trial ended inconclusively with a hung jury. The second trial delivered a guilty verdict, but justice's scales wavered, leading to the overturning of that judgment. In a more subdued setting, away from the media circus, a third trial unfolded, ultimately absolving Polly of guilt.

Despite three years of effort, the prosecution couldn't strongly prove the accused's guilt. However, many who knew Polly felt morally certain of her guilt in killing her relative and her child, despite lacking concrete evidence.

Polly's remaining days were spent in seclusion on Staten Island until her passing on May 27, 1892, age eighty-two. Her demise, however, did not exorcise the enigma that surrounded her; the murders themselves continue to defy resolution. Reports of apparitions and tales of a woman cloaked in antiquated attire cradling an infant near the graves of Emeline and Ann

Eliza Housman in Fairview Cemetery emerged among Staten Islanders. Polly Bodine's final resting place is also located in Fairview Cemetery, among the graves of her murdered relatives.

DOLLHOUSE HEIST

In the mid-nineteenth century, a notorious gang of international jewel thieves operated aboard ships between New York and Europe. Their most skilled member was a woman named Fanchon Moncare, who appeared to be a little person. Accompanied by her "governess," Ada Danforth, Fanchon used her innocent façade to charm wealthy passengers aboard the luxury liners of the time and then seize the opportunity to steal their jewelry. With an endearing babydoll that contained a hidden compartment, the women were able to smuggle their loot through customs.

In Manhattan's Chinatown, Fanchon shed her innocent act, earning the moniker "midget of the devil" for her stern demeanor and sharp business deals. However, tensions arose when a new accomplice, Magda Hamilton, joined the group. Magda's betrayal led to Fanchon's life sentence.

Magda received a shorter sentence and then married a wealthy man named Dartway Crawley, who lived in a mansion on Staten Island. Crawley went to California seeking gold shortly after their union, leaving Magda alone in the house. Fanchon Moncare died in prison, unknown to Magda.

Shortly after, Magda Hamilton Crawley was found dead, mysteriously suffocated in her bed. Legend has it that Fanchon returned from the grave and choked Magda with her doll's china head, the very doll that held the loot during their heists.

It is said that the Crawley House remains haunted—not by Magda but by Fanchon Moncare. The vengeful spirit refused to rest, haunting the mansion from within and appearing on the widow's walk, a name believed to originate from the mariners' wives who anxiously awaited their spouses' return but were left widows.

In the days of the old newspapers, one could find a syndicated cartoon, *Ripley's Believe It or Not!*, created by Robert L. Ripley. It featured oddities that fascinated folks. In the 1970s, some of these strange stories were collected in comic book anthologies. This tale was included in the Ripley anthology titled *The Devil's Midget*. From 1982 to 1986, a television show was hosted by Jack Palance, which delivered *Ripley's Believe It–Or Not!* stories.

Do you believe it—or not?

THE LADY IN WHITE

In the summer of 1963, skateboarding was a popular activity among the teenagers of Mariners Harbor in Staten Island. The country had not yet turned dark and ugly from the unfortunate events that followed that year. These skaters enjoyed the thrill of riding their wooden boards with roller skate wheels attached to the bottom near the Baron Hirsch Cemetery. Despite the cemetery being off-limits, these riders would race through the winding paths until dusk, feeling the freedom of their reckless escapades.

One evening, their fun turned scary when one of the teens fell near a tombstone and injured an arm. As the skaters gathered around to help their friend, they noticed a ghostly figure cloaked in white, slender and spectral, watching them from the shadows of the woods. The Lady in White is a legendary figure known to wander cemetery grounds, and her appearance terrified the teens. They fled, the image of the mysterious apparition ingrained in their minds.

Rumors later revealed that the Lady in White was the ghost of a young anthropology student from Columbia University who had come to Staten Island to learn about the culture and traditions of the Lenape people. Unfortunately, her journey ended in tragedy when she was brutally assaulted and murdered by someone she had hoped to learn from. The injustice of her fate cast a shadow over her memory.

Could the Lady in White, the spectral figure that haunts the cemetery, be the spirit of the young woman seeking justice and peace in the afterlife? Her tragic story echoes through the ages, reminding us of the injustices that persist long after death.

STATEN ISLAND'S MOST COMPELLING MYSTERY OF 1963

A hidden tragedy lies in the annals of New York City's lore: Staten Island's most compelling mystery of 1963. The haunting tale lingers like a phantom—the infamous account of a colossal octopus's assault on the *Cornelius G. Kolff*, a Staten Island Ferry vessel. Legend has it that on November 22, 1963, this monstrous cephalopod emerged from the depths, seizing the ferry in its gargantuan tentacles and pulling it beneath the waves, claiming the lives of four hundred unfortunate souls. Though swathed in mystery and skepticism, the story is a chilling reminder of the city's maritime lore.

Amid the collective memory of New York City's lore, this chilling tale often goes untold, eclipsed by the seismic events of a fateful day—the shocking assassination of President John F. Kennedy in Dallas. Yet here's the twist: the supposed octopus-related tragedy never transpired. It was but a fabrication, born from the inventive mind of artist Joe Reginella. Unfazed by the truth, Reginella spun an intricate hoax, complete with glossy brochures, a convincing website and a symbolic sculpture, all orchestrated to entice unsuspecting tourists to a distant corner of Staten Island in pursuit of a museum dedicated to this whimsical fish tale.

Joe Reginella is an artist known for creating elaborate hoaxes and fictional narratives often presented as historical events. The "Staten Island Ferry Disaster Memorial Museum" was fabricated to commemorate an entirely fictional event involving a ferry sinking by a giant octopus in New York Harbor in 1963. This event, though fictional, was inspired by the real-life tragedies that have occurred in the city's maritime history, adding a layer of depth and realism to Reginella's narrative.

Reginella's project, a thought-provoking blend of sculpture, storytelling and performance art, challenges our perceptions of historical events and the authenticity of the information presented to us. The Staten Island Ferry Disaster Memorial Museum featured artifacts, photographs and historical accounts of the fictitious event, all meticulously crafted by Reginella. His creative process involved extensive research into historical artifacts and accounts, which he then re-created, with meticulous attention to detail, to resemble a genuine museum exhibition.

The hoax, created by Reginella, not only garnered significant attention but also sparked a profound discussion about the blurred line between fact and fiction in historical narratives. While the elaborate setup initially deceived some, others swiftly recognized it as a work of art and appreciated its satirical commentary on the construction of historical memory. This controversial project catapulted Reginella into the spotlight, solidifying his reputation as a master of artistic deception and sparking a new wave of interest in his work.

The *Cornelius G. Kolff* was a real steam-powered ferry boat that operated for over thirty years, beginning in 1951. Despite rumors that a sea monster caused its demise, it was actually turned into a floating inmate dorm for Rikers Island by the New York City Department of Correction in 1987. The boat was eventually sold for scrap in 2003. Reginella claimed the ship had been discovered intact, and it took six months to plan the prank, which he described as "part practical joke, part multimedia art project, part social experiment."

The Staten Island ferry disaster memorial sculpture. *Courtesy of artist and creator Joe Reginella.*

Reginella's octopus hoax is a reminder to approach historical narratives critically and question the authenticity of presented information.

Joseph Reginella, a self-taught sculptor, embarked on his artistic journey at fourteen, delving into sculpture and mold-making, fueled by his passion for monsters and horror movies. Since 1994, he has exerted his talent professionally as a commercial artist, leaving his creative mark on various projects. Notably, he is the mastermind behind the Toxic Teddies toy line. He has crafted pieces for esteemed clients, such as *Harper's Bazaar* magazine, Juicy Couture, Macy's and the Children's Museum of Manhattan.

Reginella's artistic efforts have transcended boundaries, earning him global recognition through multimedia art installations showcased on his website, NYCurbanlegends.com. The *New York Times* likened him to "the Banksy of monuments," highlighting his innovative approach to art. Notably, former New York City mayor Ed Koch possessed a sculpture by Reginella, emphasizing the artist's impact on the city's cultural landscape. Among his notable works stands a poignant 9/11 statue commissioned by the Snug Harbor Cultural Museum, a testament to his ability to capture emotion and historical significance through his art.

THE GHOSTLY HITCHHIKER

The eerie tale of the ghostly hitchhiker begins innocently enough: a young woman in a flowing white dress stands out against the darkness of the night. She stands by the roadside, her form barely visible in the dim glow of passing headlights. Who is she? What does she want? These questions linger in the minds of the protagonists, a girlfriend's best friend and her father, unsuspecting travelers on this lonely stretch of road near Willowbrook State School. Their kindness prompts them to offer a ride to the mysterious hitchhiker, who claims to live just a few miles down the road. Little do they know they're about to become entangled in a tale of the supernatural. As the car glides along Victory Boulevard, the atmosphere grows increasingly tense. The young woman in white sits silently in the backseat, her presence real yet unearthly. As they approach the supposed destination, an unease settles over the travelers.

To their astonishment and growing dread, their ghostly passenger vanishes into thin air just as they reach the specified address. The car slows to a stop, the engine's hum the only sound in the night. Perplexed and unnerved, they muster the courage to knock on the door of the home and share their bizarre encounter with the residents.

What they hear sends a chill down their spines. The house's residents, their eyes wide with disbelief, recount a tale of tragedy—a daughter who once matched the description of the hitchhiker but who had vanished years ago. She, too, was last seen hitchhiking on this very road. This revelation deepens the mystery.

As the chilling realization dawns on them, the travelers can't help but feel a shiver run down their spines. Today is no ordinary day—it is the anniversary of the ghostly hitchhiker's disappearance, a day when her spectral form returns to haunt the living. And in this moment of eerie coincidence, they can't help but wonder: Did they encounter a mere apparition or something far more sinister lurking in the darkness?

THE PHANTOM JOGGERS OF WOLFE'S POND PARK

The bitterest tears shed over graves are for words left unsaid and deeds left undone.
—*Harriet Beecher Stowe*

The Phantom Jogger of Wolfe's Pond Park is a spooky tale that gives Staten Island locals goosebumps when they venture into the park after dark. The eerie legend revolves around a ghostly figure dressed in athletic clothes who appears in the late hours of the evening, moving silently along the park's winding paths. Witnesses swear they've glimpsed the phantom jogger, his form illuminated by moonlight, but they say he vanishes into the night air when he is approached.

Wolfe's Pond Park includes a scenic beach, abundant wildlife habitats, beautiful park benches dedicated to loved ones and serene plant preserves. However, underneath the park's tranquil façade, there's a darker history marked by tragedy and past misfortune.

This heartbreaking tale of loss involves a fatal car crash that claimed the lives of two young souls. Their spirits are said to haunt the park, forever tied to the spot where their lives were cut short. Locals speak in hushed tones of encountering the ghostly apparitions of these ill-fated teens, their ethereal forms moving along the pathways in the dead of night. Some even claim to hear the echo of the joggers' voices, calling out into the darkness, yearning for the comfort of their parents' embrace.

At 2:00 a.m., the witching hour arrives at Wolfe's Pond Park, and the line between the living and the dead blurs. The phantom jogger and the ghostly teens emerge at this time, reminding the park of its haunted history. Some brave souls venture into the park at this hour, hoping to catch a glimpse of the paranormal beings, while others avoid the park at all costs.

It's worth noting that urban legends stem from folklore, storytelling and imagination. While these tales may give you chills and make your heart race, their authenticity is questionable. So, embrace them as part of the rich storytelling on Staten Island, where every whispered rumor adds another layer of intrigue to the island's mystique. Nonetheless, the history of Wolfe's Pond Park remains a fascinating and intriguing part of Staten Island's past, making it a must-visit for those interested in the supernatural and the history of the area.

THE REAL ICHABOD CRANE
ICHABOD CRANE HOUSE
FORMERLY LOCATED AT 3525 VICTORY BOULEVARD

Irving's character was inspired by Colonel Ichabod Crane. This actual military official lived in Staten Island and was buried at the Asbury Cemetery in the New Springville area. The inscription on Crane's headstone reads, "Col. of the U.S. Army, who was born in Elizabeth Town, N.J., and died on Staten Island. He served his country faithfully for 48 years and was much beloved and respected by all who knew him."

Ichabod Crane is a fictional character, a gangly and unappealing schoolmaster who is the protagonist of Washington Irving's short story "The Legend of Sleepy Hollow." Ichabod Crane is relatively impoverished, and his main interest is self-advancement. He endeavors to further his cause by impressing the daughters of wealthy families with his learning. However, he is also very gullible, and his belief in ghosts and other paranormal phenomena eventually gets the better of him.

Washington Irving's story "The Legend of Sleepy Hollow" is probably best known for its villain, the Headless Horseman, who has inspired countless paintings, cartoons, movies, stage performances and other adaptations. Less famous but still well remembered is the name of the cowardly central figure in the tale, Ichabod Crane. The character, who fails to acquire the hand of the wealthy and winsome Katrina Van Tassel, is described as "lean and lanky" and is portrayed as highly superstitious. The character's name comes from a U.S. Army captain Irving met in the War of 1812, but the personage resembles the schoolmaster of Kinderhook School in Kinderhook, New York, Jesse Merwin. Merwin and Irving reportedly became friends around 1809, when Irving was staying in Kinderhook, and the two continued to correspond for decades afterward. The school, which sits on the former site of Merwin's school, is known as the Ichabod Crane School.

But who was the real Ichabod Crane, who lived and was buried in Staten Island?

The physical description of Irving's principal character, Ichabod Crane, has been seared into the memories of many Staten Islanders since childhood. He is tall and lanky, with long arms and legs and hands that dangled a mile out of his sleeves, and his feet could double as shovels. His small head was flat, and his giant ears and long, skinny nose were a sight as he strode in his baggy clothes. A scarecrow might come to mind when conjuring up his image.

The real Ichabod Crane, Ichabod Bennet Crane, however, was born in Elizabethtown, New Jersey, in 1787, fewer than fifty miles from the location of the fictitious Sleepy Hollow. Unlike Irving's portrayal, Ichabod B. Crane was not a lanky and unattractive schoolmaster. He was a challenging and seasoned military officer, a man of action and bravery. He was a courageous man who would have drawn his saber and charged the ghostly horseman rather than cowardly flee with the "skirts of his black coat flutter[ing] out almost to the horse's tail." This is the real Ichabod Crane, a man who deserves to be remembered for his bravery and service, not just as a character in a ghost story.

Ichabod B. Crane joined the U.S. Marine Corps at an early age. When the War of 1812 broke out, he accepted a commission as a captain in the U.S. Army and served as the commander of various forts along the Niagara frontier. He eventually was brevetted to the rank of major. He led troops in several campaigns, including the Black Hawk War in 1832; the Second Seminole War in 1835, when he served under future president Zachary Taylor; and, later, along the United States–Canadian border during Canada's Patriot War in 1838, ultimately rising to the rank of colonel in 1843 before the start of the Mexican-American War.

Interestingly, Washington Irving and Ichabod Crane were stationed at Fort Pike on Lake Ontario in Sackets Harbor, New York, in 1814. Irving was an aide to New York's governor, who was inspecting defenses in the area, while Crane was an artillery captain. Scholars debate whether the two met there, but in all likelihood, Irving simply learned of Crane's unusual name and recorded it for future works, as he was known to do. In so doing, Irving must have realized the career military officer would not be pleased with such a disrespectful use of his exceptional moniker.

It has been reported that Colonel Ichabod Crane did indeed resent his name being used in Irving's famous Halloween story and loathed Irving for it. After the story's publication, this military tough guy must have often suffered humiliation when introducing himself: "Oh, like the Sleepy Hollow schoolmaster?" One can only imagine his reply. It also must have been difficult hearing snickers among the ranks when troops learned of their commanding officer's name. After all, his career demanded respect, and he had earned it.

Ichabod's family had a rich history of service and achievement. His grandfather Stephen Crane was a judge who served as a delegate to the Continental Congress alongside the likes of George Washington, John and Samuel Adams and Patrick Henry. He was bayoneted in a skirmish with British troops during the American Revolutionary War and died of his wounds in 1780. Ichabod's father, William Crane, rose to the rank of brigadier general and lost a leg from wounds he suffered at the Battle of Quebec in 1775. Ichabod's brother William Crane was a naval officer in the War of 1812. Another brother, Joseph Crane, was a judge and an Ohio congressman. Ichabod's son, Charles Henry Crane, became not only a brigadier general but also a U.S. surgeon general and one of the physicians who attended to the mortally wounded Abraham Lincoln in the Petersen House. Ichabod's nephew was a major in the Army of the Potomac during the U.S. Civil War. And if that isn't enough to distinguish the Crane family, Ichabod's great-nephew Stephen Crane penned *The Red Badge of Courage* in 1895, a substantial piece of American literature more befitting of the Crane family.

The real Ichabod Crane died of natural causes in 1857—he was not "spirited away by supernatural means" like his fictitious namesake.

Yet the real Colonel Ichabod Crane is still exploited in movies, TV series and cartoons. We should ask ourselves: Which Ichabod Crane should we remember? The one who served his country faithfully for forty-eight years and was much beloved and respected by all who knew him, or the fictional character, who, though entertaining, does not accurately represent the real man?

Should Colonel Crane be grateful his name is remembered at all? The Ichabod B. Crane born in 1787 was a graduate of West Point, did a hitch in the marines and later served as an army captain in the War of 1812. After the Mexican-American War, around 1850, Crane purchased a farm on the Richmond Turnpike (now Victory Boulevard) near Signs Road in the Chelsea Heights section. Unfortunately, Crane could not enjoy his home in Richmond County for long; he died on October 5, 1857, at his home. The house at 3525 Victory Boulevard was demolished in 1989, when preservationists could not raise the money to move it to the Historic Richmond Town. Commercial buildings now occupy the site.

Remember, unlike the faint-hearted Crane from the story, this Crane was brave and courageous under fire.

AARON BURR'S RESTLESS SPIRIT

The way to love anything is to realize that it may be lost.
—Gilbert K. Chesterton

Throughout the streets and corners of New York City, stories abound of lovelorn spirits haunting the living, their ethereal presence a reminder of romance and tragedy intertwined. Most ghost tales double as love stories. Their origins often involve murder, unjust deaths or heartbreak.

For those who prefer their romance with a touch of scandal, look no further than Aaron Burr. From his infamous trial in 1799 to the fatal duel with Alexander Hamilton in 1804, Burr's life was a series of daring escapades. He even attempted to establish his own nation and faced treason charges. Burr is a reasonably active ghost around New York City and has been spotted on the battery, waiting for his daughter Theodosia's ship to come in (she was lost at sea). Burr's ghost remains active, particularly in pursuit of female company. However, he avoids the Morris-Jumel Mansion, perhaps to avoid his ex-wife Eliza's ghost. After a stint in Europe and facing financial ruin, Burr returned to New York, where he hastily wed Eliza Jumel, dubbed the "black widow," only to divorce her four months later.

The oldest surviving house in Manhattan, the Morris-Jumel Mansion, stands as a testament to the rich history of New York City and America. Constructed in 1765 for the Morris family, this historic residence occupies its original grounds, located on the ancestral homeland of the Lenape people, encompassing fifty modern city blocks. Throughout its storied past, the mansion functioned as the strategic headquarters for General Washington and later accommodated British and Hessian troops during the American Revolution. Following a brief stint as a tavern, the property was purchased by Stephen and Eliza Jumel in 1810. Following Stephen's passing, Eliza wed Aaron Burr.

In February 1804, Burr's bid for the New York governorship faced sabotage when Hamilton circulated disparaging letters about him, leading to his defeat. Subsequently, Governor Clinton replaced Burr as the Republican vice presidential candidate. This culminated in a fateful duel between Burr and Hamilton in Weehawken, New Jersey, on July 11, 1804. (Although duels were illegal in New York and New Jersey, the penalties were less severe in the latter state.) The details of the duel remain controversial. Conflicting accounts persist regarding who fired first and whether Hamilton intentionally missed or accidentally discharged his pistol after being hit by

Burr. Regardless, Burr emerged unscathed, while Hamilton suffered a fatal wound and succumbed the following day.

Burr met his end in 1836 at a boardinghouse in Staten Island's Port Richmond neighborhood near the Bayonne Bridge. This boardinghouse was later transformed into the St. James Hotel, offering guests the peculiar option to lodge in Burr's former room, even sharing his bed. A sign above the mantel chillingly proclaimed, "Aaron Burr died in this room."

In his final days, Burr secluded himself in this room, grappling with loneliness and revisiting old love letters from Eliza. Accounts from an 1895 *New York Times* article depict him as being besieged by persistent ministers, striving to alleviate his despair and secure salvation.

Adding to the eerie narrative, a mysterious visitor at the boardinghouse exhibited an unnerving fixation on Burr, silently observing him. Upon learning of Burr's demise, the stranger materialized at the door, producing the tools to craft a plaster death mask of the former vice president.

The St. James Hotel is the place where Aaron Burr died and was built shortly after the Revolutionary War, around 1787. It was demolished in 1945 and has since been replaced by an apartment complex. There is a plaque on the building marking it as the site of the St. James Hotel and the death place of Aaron Burr.

CONCLUSION

Many cultures view the belief in ghosts as a way to honor ancestors, and failure to respect these spirits may lead to haunting as retribution. Despite the lack of scientific evidence of ghosts, strange phenomena suggest their potential existence. Determining a spirit's nature—whether benevolent or malevolent—is often based on the feelings experienced in their presence. Ghostly encounters engage all the senses and include temperature changes and unusual smells. These encounters can be deeply personal, evoking memories of loved ones or the souls of individuals who perished under unfortunate circumstances. Ultimately, the belief in ghosts is a matter of individual choice, with encounters varying in nature and significance, but it is important to respect these beliefs as part of our collective cultural heritage.

In conclusion, delving into the paranormal folklore, mysteries and hoaxes of Staten Island, a borough with a rich history dating back to its Native inhabitants and later European colonization, offers more than just entertainment; it provides a unique lens through which to explore the island's rich history. Whether rooted in fact or embellished by legend, these tales serve as a means to understand the cultural, social and historical dynamics that have shaped Staten Island over the years. They offer insights into the fears, beliefs and aspirations of the island's inhabitants across different eras, reflecting the evolving fabric of society.

By studying these stories, we embark on a journey of unraveling the mysterious tales of the supernatural and uncovering hidden layers of the past.

An illustration of a man frightened as a ghostly apparition looms behind him. *NYPL Digital Collection*.

This process illuminates forgotten events, traditions and customs, enriching our understanding of Staten Island's origin and the various influences that have shaped its identity.

Ultimately, the paranormal folklore, mysteries and hoaxes of Staten Island serve as more than just tales of the inexplicable—they are windows into the collective consciousness of a community, a testament to its resilience, imagination and enduring quest for understanding. They also reflect the societal issues and anxieties of their time, such as the fear of the unknown or the desire for justice.

As we continue to unravel the mysteries of this borough, we simultaneously unearth new dimensions of its history, enriching our appreciation for the complexities of the human experience.

Researching and compiling this book has been immensely rewarding for me. I've delved deep into the subject matter, uncovering captivating stories and insights along the way. I hope you enjoyed reading it as much as I enjoyed writing it.

BIBLIOGRAPHY

Print Sources

Anarumo, Theresa, and Maureen Seaberg. *Hidden History of Staten Island.* Charleston, SC: The History Press, 2017.

Brown, Jenn. *Abandoned New York: The Forgotten Beauties.* Charleston, SC: America Through Time, 2019.

Capo, Fran. *New York Myths and Legends.* Essex, CT: Globe Pequot, 2019.

Farnsworth, Cheri. *The Big Book of New York Ghost Stories.* Essex, CT: Globe Pequot, 2019.

Gethard, Chris, Mark Moran, et al. *Weird New York: Your Guide to New York's Local Legends and Best Kept Secrets.* New York: Union Square & Co., 2010.

Gold, Kenneth M. *The Forgotten Borough: Staten Island and the Subway.* New York: Columbia University Press, 2023.

Holzer, Hans. *Houses of Horror.* New York: Fall River Press, 2012.

Illustrated Sketch Book of Staten Island, New York, Its Industries and Commerce. New York: S.C. Judson, 1886. Library of Congress. tile.loc.gov/ storage-services/public/gdcmassbookdig/illustratedsketc00juds/ illustratedsketc00juds.pdf.

Lundrigan, Margaret, and Tova Navarra R.N. *Staten Island.* Charleston, SC: Arcadia Publishing, 1997.

Macken, Lynda Lee. *Haunted History of Staten Island.* Edmonton, CA: Black Cat Press, 2000.

Nese, Marco, and Francesco Nicotra. *Antonio Meucci 1808–1889.* Rome, IT: n.p., 1989.

Ocker, J.W. *The New York Grimpendium: A Guide to Macabre and Ghastly Sites in New York State.* Woodstock, VT: Countryman Press, 2012.

Salmon, Patricia. *Murder and Mayhem on Staten Island.* Charleston, SC: The History Press, 2013.

————. *Staten Island Slayings: Murderers & Mysteries of the Forgotten Borough.* Charleston, SC: The History Press, 2014

Salmon, Patricia, and Barnett Shepherd. *The Staten Island Ferry: A History.* Staten Island, NY: Staten Island Museum, 2008.

Articles, Online Resources and Web Content

Abandoned NYC. "Ghosts of Kreischerville." www.abandonednyc.com/2017/01/09/ghosts-of-kreischerville/.

Blue Belt Conservancy. "The History of Brady's Pond...thru the Years." thebluebeltconservancy.weebly.com/pastpresent-and-future.html.

Broad, William J. "How the Ice Age Shaped New York." *New York Times*, June 5, 2018. https://www.nytimes.com/2018/06/05/science/how-the-ice-age-shaped-new-york.html.

Buiso, Gary. "9/11 Rubble Haunted by Female Ghost: Book." *New York Post*, March 15, 2015. https://nypost.com/2015/03/15/911-rubble-haunted-by-female-ghost-book/.

Castello, William J. "The Art of William J Castello." www.wmjcastelloart.net.

City of New York. "New York City Farm Colony—Seaview Hospital, Historic District, Designation Report." Landmarks Preservation Commission. 1985. https://s-media.nyc.gov/agencies/lpc/lp/1408.pdf.

Clemens, Will M. "The Staten Island Mystery of 1843." *Era* 14 (July 1904): n.p.

Bosco, James. "Staten Island, Forgotten Borough." *Current Affairs*, April 3, 2023. www.currentaffairs.org/2023/04/staten-island-forgotten-borough.

Design Inspirationalist. "Inspiration Photo Friday: Time to Explore." www.thedesigninspirationalist.com/tag/seaview-hospital/.

Ephemeral New York. "Buffalo Bill's Wild West Show Thrills 1894 Brooklyn." July 17, 2017. https://ephemeralnewyork.wordpress.com/2017/07/17/buffalo-bills-wild-west-show-thrills-1894-brooklyn/.

Find a Grave. "Ichabod Bennett Crane." https://www.findagrave.com/memorial/7304801/ichabod-bennett-crane.

GhostQuest USA. "Top 13 Most Haunted Places in Staten Island, New York." YouTube. https://www.youtube.com/watch?v=DE2aVgqqUv4.

Haunted Rooms. "Staten Island Haunts." www.hauntedrooms.com.

Jelly-Schapiro, Joshua. "How New York Was Named." *New Yorker*, April 13, 2021. www.newyorker.com/books/page-turner/how-new-york-was-named.

La Gorce, Tammy. "What Door-to-Door Tradition Came Before Trick-or-Treating?" *New York Times*, October 21, 2016. www.nytimes.com/2016/10/23/nyregion/what-door-to-door-tradition-came-before-trick-or-treating.html.

Lane, Doris. "The Cruser Family Burying Ground: A Most Abandoned Cemetery." Friends of Abandoned Cemeteries Inc. www.nygenweb.net/richmond/facsi/newsletters/facsivol14no1.html.

Lantern Ghost Tours. "Was There a Ghost in One of America's Most Famous Landfill Sites?" January 14, 2021. https://www.lanternghosttours.com/post/was-there-a-ghost-in-one-of-america-s-most-famous-landfill-sites.

Leek, Sybil. "Equestrian History Fades Here." March 2011. www.silive.com.

Library of Congress. "Annals of Staten Island, from Its Discovery to the Present Time." tile.loc.gov/storage-services/public/gdcmassbookdig/annalsofstatenis00clut/annalsofstatenis00clut.pdf.

Lost Destinations. "New York." www.lostdestinations.com.

Mae, Tara. "Alice Austin: Audacious Artist." Three Village Historical Society. November 8, 2020. www.threevillagehistoricalsociety.org/post/alice-austen-audacious-artist.

National Library of Medicine. "U.S. Army. Halloran General Hospital, Staten Island, N.Y." collections.nlm.nih.gov/catalog/nlm:nlmuid-101402103-img.

National Park Service. "A Detailed History of Miller Field." February 26, 2015. www.nps.gov/gate/learn/historyculture/detailsmillerfield.htm.

Neves, Gabriel. "Top 10 Secrets of St. George on Staten Island." Untapped New York. https://untappedcities.com/2022/03/15/secrets-st-george-staten-island/4/.

New York Haunted Houses. "Haunted History of St. Andrews Church." www.newyorkhauntedhouses.com.

New York Post. "Mom Killed by Falling Headstone in Staten Island Cemetery." February 19, 2022.

New York Public Library Digital Collections. "Staten Island Post Cards." digitalcollections.nypl.org/collections/staten-island-post-cards.

New York Times. "Bombs Found in the Bay. Cause a Panic Among Employees of Staten Island Shipyard." October 1, 1907. https://timesmachine.nytimes.com/timesmachine/1907/10/01/104708815.pdf.

———. "Obituary for BENJAMIN PRINE." October 5, 1900. https://www.newspapers.com/article/the-new-york-times-obituary-for-benjamin/117824558/.

———. "President Scores 'Virus of Bigotry'—Warns It Must Be Stemmed as Peril to Freedom." January 13, 1960.

NYCData. "Infrastructure: New York City (NYC), Fresh Kills—Staten Island." https://www.baruch.cuny.edu/nycdata/infrastructure/freshkills.html.

NYC Urban Legends. "Joseph Reginella." nycurbanlegends.com.

———. "Staten Island Urban Legends." www.nycurbanlegends.com.

Old Dutch Church NYC. "Battle in a Blizzard—January 15, 1780." www.olddutchchurchnyc.org/battle-of-january-15-1780.

PastPerfect Online. "Staten Island." www.pastperfectonline.com.

Pitanza, Kristin. "This Way on Bay: Did You Know Ichabod Crane Was Buried on Staten Island?" This Way on Bay. April 13, 2016. https://thiswayonbay.com/staten-island-history-ichabod-crane/.

Power 97.3 WBLK. "Deadly Plane Crashes In New York." https://wblk.com/deadliest-plane-crashes-ny.

Revolutionary War Staten Island. "A Hessian View of the British Troops at Staten Island." August 29, 2019. https://revolutionarywarstatenisland.com/2019/08/29/a-hessian-view-of-the-british-troops-at-staten-island/.

Rizzi, Nicholas. "Ghost Hunters Will Try to Track Spirits at Garibaldi's Staten Island Home." DNAinfo. October 24, 2012. www.dnainfo.com/new-york/20121024/rosebank/ghost-hunters-will-try-track-spirits-at-garibaldis-staten-island-home/.

Someone Lived Here. "Alice Austen House." www.someonelivedhere.com/ep1-alice-austen-house/.

St. George Theatre. "Architecture." www.stgeorgetheatre.com.

Towner, Myriah. "What Did They Do with the Debris from 9/11?" Daily Mail, March 15, 2015. https://www.dailymail.co.uk/news/article-2995782/NYPD-cop-saw-ghost-searching-clues-identify-World-Trade-Center-victims-searched-9-11-debris-landfill-book-reveals.html.

Travel Channel. "Ghost Adventures: Sailors' Snug Harbor Pictures." www.travelchannel.com/shows/ghost-adventures/photos/ghost-adventures-sailors-snug-harbor-pictures.

True Warrior Jewelry. www.truewarriorjewelry.com.

Untapped New York. "Eerie Landscape of Abandoned Mariner's Marsh on Staten Island." https://untappedcities.com/2014/11/21/the-10-best-podcasts-based-in-nyc-from-radiolab-this-american-life-to-the-combat-jack-show/.

Vice. "How One Playground Horror Story Reached Millions of Children Around the World." www.vice.com/en/article/k78njy/bloody-mary-myth-horror-story.

Village Historical Society. "Alice Austen: Audacious Artist." www.threevillagehistoricalsociety.org/post/alice-austen-audacious-artist.

Weird U.S. "The Ghosts of Historic Richmondtown." www.weirdus.com/states/new_york/ghosts/richomond_town/index.php.

Werewoofs. "Haunted Staten Island." www.werewoofs.com.

YouTube. "The Brooklyn Bridge Elephant Stampede." www.youtube.com/watch?v=F1-9SkUj2DE.

———. "Camps & a Mysterious Auto Graveyard!" www.youtube.com/watch?v=2GFY3HenbS0.

———. "Cropsey and the Missing Children (Urban Legend Documentary) | Real Stories." www.youtube.com/watch?v=Zl4-jfDQanY.

———. "Exploring Staten Island...Creepy Abandoned Buildings, Forgotten Camps & a Mysterious Auto Graveyard!" www.youtube.com/watch?v=2GFY3HenbS0.

———. "The Haunted Bayley Seton Hospital, Staten Island, NY." www.youtube.com/watch?v=LZIhBgQvay8.

———. "Murder on the High Seas of Staten Island." www.youtube.com/watch?v=ENOJlYtXrd4.

———. "Staten Island's Nightmare: The Urban Legend That Turned Out to Be Real." www.youtube.com/watch?v=owHboDoQNbE.

———. "Why Hundreds of New York Ships Were Abandoned on Staten Island." www.youtube.com/watch?v=6CXIvjxtAxE.

About the Author

Marianna Randazzo, an author and educator, blends her experiences growing up in an Italian American household in Brooklyn, New York, and her nearly two decades as a Staten Islander into her diverse literary works. Despite her time spent living in Staten Island, she humorously acknowledges that she may never be considered a true native.

Drawing from her time as a schoolteacher, reading specialist and adjunct professor, she brings depth to her writing, shaped by years of engaging with diverse audiences. Her adventures with her late husband, traveling and exploring paranormal sites, influenced her storytelling and her respect for the supernatural.

Marianna's literary prowess has been recognized with prestigious awards such as the OSDIA Literary Award, the Morgagni Society Silver Medal Award and the Garibaldi-Meucci Museum Recognition Award. Her contributions to preserving and promoting literature and Italian American heritage have been lauded by esteemed government bodies, including the New York State Assembly, New York City Council and a Richmond County district attorney, borough president and state senator. This recognition is a testament to the impact of her work.

Marianna is the author of *Given Away: A Sicilian Upbringing, 10th Anniversary Edition*; *Italians of Brooklyn* (Arcadia Publishing, 2018); *Father Vincent R.*

Capodanno, Navy Chaplain; and *Michael Behette: Brooklyn's Best.* She has also penned hundreds of parenting and educational articles for various publications over the years. To learn more about her work, visit her website at www.marianna-randazzo.com.